LIVING THE SKY LIFE

BARBARA BORZI

Copyright © 2021 by Barbara Borzi

All rights reserved.

No part of this book may be reproduced in any form or by any electronic or mechanical means, including information storage and retrieval systems, without written permission from the author, except for the use of brief quotations in a book review.

❦ Created with Vellum

Disclaimer

The stories in this book reflect the author's recollection of events. Some locations and identifying characteristics have been changed to protect the privacy of those depicted. Dialogue has been recreated from memory. Now sit back, relax, and enjoy the flight. What you're about to learn is not taught or endorsed by any training school.

***Dedicated to my parents who would always tell me
I had my head in the clouds.***

Sempre con la testa nelle nuvole.

The flight attendant smile—fooling passengers since 1912.

— *ANONYMOUS*

CONTENTS

Chapter 1	1
Chapter 2	20
Chapter 3	32
Chapter 4	40
Chapter 5	58
Chapter 6	67
Chapter 7	77
Chapter 8	94
Chapter 9	117
Chapter 10	126
Chapter 11	136
Chapter 12	153
Chapter 13	158
Chapter 14	170
Acknowledgements	179
About the Author	181

Chapter One

The Gift

My fate had been sealed the moment my parents had bought me a service trolley when I was five years old. It had become tradition among my relatives to take turns annually hosting Christmas, and this year had been my family's turn. This meant I would have to wait until everyone (nine people) had arrived before I could tear open the big, meticulously wrapped gift that I had already spotted under the tree with my name on it. My mother had me wear one of the dresses she had made, which was no surprise because all I owned were handmade dresses. I never even owned pants until I came home from school complaining that everyone else was wearing pants. The following week I was given ugly hand-me-downs—just what I was hoping for. Thankfully, I didn't have to wear the usual white lace knee-high socks that Italian moms used to always make their daughters wear. They were itchy and would leave a pattern on my legs, but on this day, I wore regular cotton knee-highs. My mother had brushed my hair and clipped the side back with my favourite yellow butterfly barrette. Even though the aroma coming from my mom's homemade lasagna cooking in the oven was making my stomach growl, I was ready and eager to start the gift opening.

The adults decided my cousins, brother, and I had suffered enough and finally let us open our gifts before sitting down for lunch. *What can it be? What can it be?* I thought gleefully. Anything this big had to be awesome! It was a pale yellow, two-tiered plastic serving trolley on wheels. The second my dad had it assembled I was throwing everything I could find on it so I could make a buck. The TV remote control, my mom's cigarettes, a pen, a box of tissues—if you wanted it, you had to pay for it. Ingenious. My parents let me grab items around the house and then sell them back to them. I was only charging pennies mind you, but for a five-year-old this meant I was one step closer to that bubble gum machine in the mall. I think the point of the cart was to serve beverages, such as tea, (at no profit —how dumb was that?) but I liked my way much better. I was an entrepreneurial flight attendant in the making.

My first real experience of life in an airport happened from the ages of eighteen to twenty-one. I held a part-time job working in a retail store at the airport selling various handmade items from the Northwest Territories. I used to watch the terminal come alive as early as 0600 hours as I'd be opening the store, watch the hustle and bustle of passengers passing by, and I even met some remarkably interesting people. Many of the customers in my store were the business travellers who hadn't bought anything while in town and needed to pick something up at the last minute before heading home to their families. Who knew that seventeen years after receiving a service trolley for Christmas, I'd find myself being interviewed for a flight attendant position? Like many other university graduates, I held a degree but had no clue what I was supposed to do with it. I held a specialization in history and a major in French literature. This basically meant I enjoyed four years of storytelling. So, what does one do when they enjoy school and don't know what career to pursue? They continue with yet more schooling.

I now found myself engaged in a French translation and interpretation program. While in this program, I managed to land my first full-time job. Working part time did not provide enough funds to cover the cost of education as well as clothing and entertainment. (This nerd also liked to date and have fun.) My new job was with an airline as a customer sales and service agent. After my six-month probationary period, I experienced my first taste of standby travel.

Ten of us newbies from the office decided it would be fun to travel to Los Angeles (LAX) for our first standby flight with the company. We all agreed to meet in LAX on a specific day. I flew in on the first flight that morning and met up with the group. We became part of the audience on *The Price Is Right* show and then ran over to join *The Tonight Show* audience. None of us became rich or famous that day, but it was a fast, fun-packed adventure that I would repeat again in a heartbeat. Later that evening I flew home with places racing through my head of where I'd head to next.

Halifax (YHZ) was my next one-day adventure but this time with my father. The two of us flew out for the day to visit my brother, who was attending St. Mary's University. He showed us around campus and downtown, and then we went home after dinner. It probably would have been more fun if it wasn't winter and there weren't so many hills.

Fredericton (YFC) was a bit of a blur. It was a full flight out, but my boyfriend had managed to get the last cabin seat while I sat in the cockpit with the pilots. We visited our friend who was attending university there. We might have had a few drinks and might have caused a bit of a disturbance at a local bar playing vicious air hockey and accidentally putting holes in walls, but if you had interrogated me, I would've pleaded the Fifth. We stayed overnight at his dorm and left first thing in the morning (at least I thought it was morning . . .).

Zurich (ZRH) was my first standby travel that was longer than one night. My boyfriend and I flew out for two weeks, travelling through Switzerland and Italy on the Eurail. This was a discounted ticket I was able to obtain through my company, which included unlimited train travel between five different countries for two weeks. We visited numerous tourist cities and stayed with some of my relatives in Brescia and Como in Italy. It was an amazing opportunity that I was grateful we took advantage of because this was the last time I would ever see my grandparents.

In Quebec City (YQB), my boyfriend and I were greeted by a hailstorm on our way to the hotel. During our one day there we visited Old Quebec City and helped ourselves to a free buffet dinner being served in our hotel. Okay, so there might have been a private function happening, but no one stopped us as we carried our plates full of food up to our room.

I had officially gotten hit by the "travel bug." City names had now morphed into airport codes, and I could recite the phonetic alpha through Zulu alphabet (to be explained in greater detail later in the book) like nobody's business.

The only problem was that as much as I was enjoying the travel perks, I was detesting the job itself. It entailed sitting in front of a computer and answering calls made by irate customers all day long. Most of the calls would start with something like, "Do you know how long I've been waiting on the phone for?!" and then just escalate from there. I once had a customer who had fallen asleep waiting and was snoring when I had answered. There was a red button on our phones that would flash if there were more than one hundred calls waiting. The only time I didn't see the flashing was when I purposely placed a sticky note over it. It was especially annoying when I'd look over to where the "dinosaurs" were seated, and they'd be laughing with one another and filing their nails. The dinosaurs were, quite frankly, old. Their job was the same as mine, except they had been with the company for so long that they could not be touched. They were the endangered species that no one dared to mess with. Even though none of the cubicles in the office were reserved, we newbies knew better than to sit in the dinosaurs' area. This area was in the most ideal location, next to the windows, nonetheless.

I had grown to hate my job so much that it would physically make me nauseous on the subway ride over just thinking about it. I would think about the screen flashing at me when a problematic customer would call back again after having already spoken to someone else. (We could write notes on customer files but also enable it to flash as a warning to the next unfortunate agent who had to deal with the same person.) I would think about the number of times I had to tell people, "no, you cannot make any changes to your ticket," and then have to stop myself from saying, "because you bought the cheapo fare." As much as I enjoyed the travel privileges, it wasn't worth sacrificing my sanity. The morning I had answered my first call to the sounds of a heavy breather, I knew I had had enough. He thought he had called a sex hotline, but from what I had heard, he was already ahead of the game. I promised myself that if I still dreaded the job by my one-year anniversary with the company, I would call it quits.

Every morning while having breakfast I would look in the wanted section of the newspaper (after reading the comics of course) in my search for a new job. As my one-year date approached, I saw an ad from another airline looking for flight attendants. I knew this had to be a sign. Without any hesitation I immediately decided to attend the cattle call. Nowadays I Google the crap out of things I'm not familiar with, but since it was 1997, Google searching was not yet a thing. I would have to rely on my charm, wit, and airline experience even though I was an introvert who had no idea this airline I was applying to even existed.

On the day of my interview, I wore a navy, two-piece business skirt suit, which my mother had previously made for me during my I-want-to-look-professional phase. The interview process began in a banquet hall along with hundreds of other applicants. It was a large, carpeted room with metal folding chairs set in numerous rows. The mix of perfume smells reminded me of walking through the beauty hall of a department store. It was better than the other smells that could permeate in a crowded room with nervous strangers, but it was still a little overwhelming. I managed to sandwich myself between two young, beautiful girls, both wearing their hair up in a bun, which made me question my choice in leaving my hair down but then quickly dismissed this thought. I was never great at styling hair, so my bun would have looked more like a tumbleweed.

As I looked around, it seemed like we were all just anxiously awaiting instructions. *How are they ever going to weed through all of us in one day?* As if on cue, someone in charge then made an announcement, "If anyone here cannot speak French, they can now leave." *Woohoo!* My French degree was now proving its worthiness. I remained seated as I watched countless sad faces stand up and exit while I rejoiced in silence. Much of what happened after that was a blur. There was some sort of a written test given to us in smaller groups, followed by an individual interview conducted first in French and then in English by a select group of interviewers. I don't remember when I was told to attend a medical screening, but I do remember going to speak to my manager at my present job with my letter of resignation in hand before even knowing if I had been selected or not at the other airline. Either way, it was time for me to quit.

The day I had announced my resignation to my manager felt so impersonal.

"Excuse me, do you have a minute?" I asked through the open door leading to her office with my letter in hand.

"Sure, come on in," she motioned.

I was never one for small talk or beating around the bush, so I simply said, "I'd like to hand in my letter of resignation."

"What's your employee number?" she asked, hardly even bothering to look up from her computer.

And with that I knew she didn't even know my name or cared to know why I was quitting. I walked out feeling relieved about the decision I had made. As I was walking back to my cubicle, a colleague told me that I'd live to regret that decision. "Maybe not today or tomorrow," he said, "but ten years from now you'll be sorry you left." He couldn't have been more wrong.

After a month of intense training with a new airline, I was awarded my wings. I figured this would be a great gig for a year or so until I could figure out what I *actually* wanted to do in life. But, like so many other flight attendants who were simply looking for a fun and exciting temporary job, the skies had sucked me in. I was a lifer. (I never did end up completing that French translation and interpretation program, by the way. When you find yourself having to down a beer at the campus pub before heading to class just to get through it, you know it's just not meant for you.)

The only thing I knew about flying before flight attendant training was that it made me sick. Literally. I always vomitted every time I flew somewhere. *Curse my weak stomach!* I knew I would have to get over this, but what I didn't realize was all the other "side effects" associated with the job, the lingo, the "special" passengers, the numerous peeves and challenges I would discover, and the world of layovers. Even though the job came with these "side effects," I found my career in the skies to be enjoyable and one I wouldn't ever trade. If you're looking for some enlightenment into life in the skies, you've come to the right place. I've got twenty-four years' worth of knowledge, experience, and stories to share. You're welcome. If you're already a sky worker or have been one, I'm sure you can relate to just about everything I've seen and experienced, and I hope you find this entertaining. And if you're neither, stick around anyway—you've already paid for the book so you might as well read it.

The Flight Attendant

Being a flight attendant used to command respect and admiration. You'd see them marching down the halls of the airports all in sync in their pristine uniforms, hardly even noticing that their path was cleared as if some big, intimidating security guard were leading them. As all eyes would rest upon them and silence would ensue, all you could hear was their parade of thrumming, rolling luggage. Not ever in my twenty-four-year reign as a flight attendant did I feel so important, so glamorous, so revered.

Here was my reality: like a toddler who had just lost her mother in a crowd of strangers, I would try to figure out which gate I needed to get to while trying to remember which destination I was headed to. I tried to blend in, but my uniform was a dead giveaway. Being an introvert, I preferred not to talk to anyone. Not that I hated people, but the energy I would require on board the aircraft to shine would be draining enough, so I needed to strategize and not waste energy on the ground. The uniform meant people knew I worked there. They could *technically* ask me questions, and questions were energy drainers. I'd then need to be alone to recharge, but that would be impossible since I was just starting work. *Run*, I would repeat to myself, *don't make eye contact!* I was alone in a jungle and I had to quickly find my herd.

"Excuse me, miss," I remember looking back to see an elderly gentleman waiting for my acknowledgement. I was caught. "Can you tell me where my gate is?" he asked, showing me his boarding card.

Okay, this would be easy, I thought. "Just follow the signs to the C gates, past duty-free." This question only required minor energy drainage. I was still okay, but then I heard, "Excuse me, miss." I continued to walk.

Much has changed over the years with not only the way flight attendants were perceived, but also in terms of their physical and emotional classification. The role of a flight attendant pre-1970s was limited to young, attractive, single women whose weight was kept under scrutiny. Once they chose to marry and have children, they no longer qualified or fit the criteria, and therefore it meant that their career was typically short-lived.

Nowadays flight attendants came in all shapes, sizes, and genders. As long as they passed a medical, they were not discriminated against. The medical exam was to rule out drug usage as well as any health conditions not conducive to flying, such as hypertension, epilepsy, asthma, or diabetes. The height and weight restrictions, still in place today, were strictly to ensure that they could safely and efficiently carry out their duties, which included being able to properly fit in the jump seat, climb through the emergency window exits, and reach into the overhead bins for emergency equipment. Generally, most flight attendants had to be between 5'3" and 6'1" but this varied according to the airline.

A flight attendant still had to conform to uniform standards but even these have become more lax over the years. When I first started with the airline, no tattoos could be visible, only one piercing per ear lobe was permitted, and high heels were deemed mandatory for women. With the changing of the times, the uniform policies lightened. Tattoos became acceptable, if not deemed offensive, piercings were no longer limited to just the ear lobes or to just one per ear, and high heels were no longer mandatory. Neck scarves were still worn, however, and nails still needed to be well manicured. Nails could not be so long as to impede the ability to perform even the simplest task, and only certain shades of polish were permitted. Hair had to still be worn up if it fell below the collar line. The addition of wearing a safety vest outside the aircraft was now imposed as part of the uniform at certain destinations. Not exactly the glamorous look. The impeccable, flawless flight attendant of yesteryears had been left in the past (along with my uniform's former shoulder pads—thank goodness!).

As much as flight attendants have physically changed in appearance, they still presented themselves as independent and confident. Whether they truly were or not was unbeknownst to others, as they have also mastered the art of faking it. The smile was one of the most revered tricks of the trade. The notorious flight attendant smile, much like that of the *Mona Lisa*, was full of ambiguities. As much as they dressed alike, smiled a lot and, for the most part, seemed friendly, what was really behind that smile and being said behind that galley curtain?

Using that flight attendant smile sometimes required a bit of acting talent as well, but if a smile was all that was needed to put someone at ease, then you confidently showed off those pearly whites. Confidence was contagious, and this was never more evident than during turbulence when all eyes would be on the flight attendants to make sure there was nothing out of the ordinary happening and all was under control. Even when I felt nauseous from the continuous rocking motion and knew the second that seat belt sign turned off I'd have to beeline for the lavatories (lavs), I'd still manage to put on a smile.

Acting included not rolling my eyes every time a passenger asked for a diet pop, knowing all too well that this would hold up my beverage service since pouring diet drinks took *so* long. (Diet drinks are fizzier than regular ones due to their lack of sugar.) It also meant not judging the other crew members who I had to sometimes work with from a different base even though I knew my base did things better. Not judging the newbies when they were on a shadow flight* (please refer to the end of each chapter for definitions of flight terminology) required a little more skill. Not because they were young and lacked experience but because I myself was never given the opportunity of a "trial run," and it reminded me of never having gotten properly trained when I worked for my husband.

I believe this needed a little backstory. I was in university at the time and looking for a part-time job. My mother suggested I send my resumé to a nearby retail company because it was so large, and she figured they probably hired many employees. Although I didn't particularly like the mall the store was in and so didn't want to apply, she insisted, and I appeased her. The interviewer (who I thought was kind of cute) gave me the job within minutes. It was my easiest interview ever. (He later told me it was the yellow canary suit that I wore that won him over, but I was fairly certain he was love struck.)

Before I knew it, I was working on the sales floor. This cute guy who hired me just threw me to the wolves with only basic training. I couldn't even work the cash register and had to rely on others to show me. On one of his sprints past me (he was always in a rush), he asked me to make a display with boxes of candied popcorn, only to later return to say he changed his mind and had me completely rearrange what I had been working on for the past two hours. He used the excuse of my being a seasonal helper to have me terminated but then wanted to date me. Being the passive-aggressive person I was, I later married this cute guy and became *his* boss.

Cute boss (future hubby)

Constantly surrounded by different crew members and passengers, flight attendants needed to be adaptable to the multitude of personalities, and as such, there were many sides to being a flight attendant. Stepping onto an airplane would sometimes feel like stepping into the twilight zone—you'd never know what to expect or who you'd meet. Would today be the day I played nurse, babysitter, superhero, custodian, mediator, negotiator, psychiatrist, police officer, or mechanic? I've held all these roles at some point or another, but what I most preferred was being my chameleon self.

For simplicity's sake, I've broken down the many faces of flight attendants into animal distinctions. At the top of this food chain, we had the lions. These were the aggressive, ferocious, angry-when-provoked flight attendants. They would eat you up and spit you out before you even had a chance to defend yourself. These were the ones you wanted around in case of an unruly passenger on board. These lions meant business. When the flight director was a lion, things got done. Period. No one dared to mess with them. The problem arose, however, when there were two lions in the crew, particularly if it was a flight director and a flight attendant. Neither one would want to relinquish control, which could sometimes lead to bloodshed. I was privy to such a spectacle once between two lions. It got ugly.

The fight started over something as simple as an orange, but because these individuals were both lions, that orange might as well have been a fat juicy steak. We were in the middle of meal service when the lion flight director chose to give an orange to a passenger who had forgotten to order a special meal for herself. She required something gluten-free, and since the regular passenger meals had gluten, the flight director saw no harm in giving away fruit from the galley. The crew were provided with individual meals, snacks, and a fruit/veggie tray to share during the flight. Most of the times, this food would end up getting wasted, as the flight attendants tended to bring their own, more nutritious options. Nonetheless, it was still common practice to ask the entire crew if it was okay to give something away to non-crew.

"Where did you get that orange?" asked the lion flight attendant to the flight director from across the aisle. She and I were handing out meals on the opposite side when she noticed the flight director leave her trolley partner and come back with the fruit.

"It's for a passenger," said the flight director while handing it to the gluten-free passenger sitting in the middle seat.

Not having gotten the answer she was looking for, she asked again, "But *where* did you get it?"

I could see the hairs starting to rise and the claws emerging. I could sense the passengers around us starting to tense in anticipation of a fight. The woman now holding the orange was attempting to hand it back, but the flight director refused and instead, lashed back at the other lion. What was said at this point, I do not know because the lions switched to a different language, but whatever they were saying involved a lot of hand gesturing and angry facial expressions. The thing about flight attendants was that most were multilingual and could easily transition into a different language when needed. Having two lions on board was sometimes just embarrassing.

Next, we had the honey badgers. These bad-ass flight attendants just didn't care. They would do what they wanted, when they wanted, and how they wanted to do it. The lion might roar at them, and, without any confrontation, they would simply go on their merry way as if nothing happened. This sometimes left the lion surprised, but he or she respected the honey badger, nonetheless. The honey badger could not be relied on, however, since they selfishly would only think about themselves and their own needs.

The sheep tended to be the less experienced flight attendants. They were sweet, gentle, non-violent, and peaceful. And, like sheep in the animal world, they were the followers. Everyone enjoyed working with sheep because they would do what they were told. After a few years, however, the sheep tended to morph into one of the other animals listed.

The sloths were obviously the slow ones. No one could really get mad at them though because they were such gentle creatures. There was usually at least one sloth per crew. The sloths tended to be so slow since they *actually* liked people and therefore wanted to talk to everyone.

The giant pandas looked cute and cuddly and, for the most part, were quite content being left alone. They knew how to defend themselves when attacked but would prefer avoiding confrontation if possible. If the giant panda was well fed, all was good.

The monkeys were extremely sociable. They enjoyed showing off and liked goofing around and playing with everyone. They were smart, witty, and full of confidence. Sometimes their overzealous nature would annoy the other animals, however.

Finally, we had the chameleons. They would try to blend in to not be noticed. They would adapt to their surroundings and would much rather be the observers than the instigators. I was a proud chameleon.

I used to work on aircraft that had a lower galley. The flight attendant who was fortunate enough to work in this galley was able to escape the hustle and bustle in the main cabin and essentially become invisible to the passengers. Once in the galley I was able to switch to running shoes for the duration of the flight because I would only appear in the cabin to use the lavatory or sit in my jump seat. It was an ideal location for a chameleon like me. The lower galley housed all the service trolleys, and it was that flight attendant's job to send up the correctly assembled trolley, or any other required item stored downstairs, at the appropriate time by ways of two one-person elevators. The lower galley had a speaker through which the crew could communicate. It was so muffled, however, that sometimes I would just relay up whatever I thought sounded right. My colleagues would eventually write notes to send down the elevator with their requests. Even though the level of communication wasn't great, it was a nice break from serving.

The problem arose when there was turbulence. Everything had to be stored and secured during this time. When that seat belt sign would chime on in the middle of meal service, a mad rush of chaos would ensue. My flight to Cuba had been particularly troublesome. It was a relatively short flight, but we were still serving hot meals to all the passengers at the time, and because of the constant need to buckle up and take our seats due to turbulence, we were on a time crunch. There were moments the thunderstorms we were attempting to fly through would be jolting our plane. As soon as the turbulence would seem to let up, we would remove our seat belts in an attempt to finish our services, but soon enough, we would be right back in our jump seats going through yet more turbulence. Carts would be sent down the elevators as quickly as possible, and I would have to remove everything off the top of them, latch all the canisters, and scramble to secure the trolleys onto "mushrooms" (not the kind you eat—you'll understand what I mean shortly). Then I would rush upstairs, possibly assist with the passenger seat-belt checks in the cabin, buckle up in my jump seat, and await the seat belt sign to turn off. This entire process would repeat itself back to back on the same flight, on many occasions.

The dreaded mushrooms required an explanation. A mushroom was flight attendant talk for those little metal things resembling mushrooms that were pulled out of the galley floor to secure a service trolley. The trolley had to fit exactly right, or it wouldn't lock into place. So here you had this big, heavy trolley that needed to roll perfectly onto a one-inch mushroom, and it needed to be done blindly because you could not see underneath the cart without physically bending over on your hands and knees, ear to the floor. Needless to say, it was no small feat. By the time you'd finally get all the carts properly secured, the turbulence would be over. These mushrooms were the bane of my existence. Besides the mushrooms and the muffled speakers, the lower galley proved to be a nice little reprieve from passenger service duties.

Unfortunately, I only had the pleasure of working on those aircraft for a few years until they were retired. The other aircraft I worked on did not have any getaways. To try to get a little "me time" I would sometimes attempt the fast-as-lightning dash down the aisles, the hard-of-hearing look, the sorry-too-occupied and the no-making-direct-eye-contact moves. These moves still proved effective on virgin or infrequent travellers but not on the experienced ones. Being an introvert, I cherished my chameleon role and did what I could to protect it.

When in uniform a flight attendant's every move and expression was being scrutinized by their passengers. Therefore, regardless of which animal a crew member might have been, being able to exude a happy, calm, and confident demeanour would help put a passenger at ease. Hence the smile. Something so simple allowed the passengers to open up about everything. When I was walking down the aisle an elderly lady, probably in her eighties, gently grabbed my arm and asked if I could assist her.

"I don't know how to read," she whispered to me when I kneeled next to her. She pulled out her customs declaration form from her seat pocket, which we had handed out at the beginning of the flight to fill out before landing.

"Not a problem," I assured her. I asked her the questions on the card and filled it out for her leaving her only to sign it. Unlike my grandmother who used to sign her name with an X because she, too, couldn't read, this passenger had been taught her signature. As she slowly formed the squiggly lines to her name, she couldn't stop thanking me for my help.

A smile meant passengers felt comfortable mingling in the back galley with the crew asking questions, such as what our favourite destination was or if we knew their friend so and so because she was also a flight attendant, or even making common jokes that we had heard many times before but pretending we hadn't. Sometimes we had returning passengers who would remember us and expect us to remember them as well even though we had served hundreds of passengers since seeing them. A smile and a nod of acknowledgement was all that was needed to make that passenger feel special.

As much as I wanted nothing more than to make my passengers happy, sometimes I just needed to take a break. When trapped in a plane travelling at

38,000 feet, however, my options were limited. There was no going outside for a smoke (not that I smoked) or getting some fresh air, and you could forget about an actual lunch break. If you did manage to sit in an actual seat and not on a bar canister in the middle of the galley because all the seats were full and your crew seats were given away to revenue passengers, you could not simply ignore a passenger standing right next to you asking for a glass of water. "Sure thing," you would politely respond as you pushed aside the meal you had been attempting to eat for the past twenty minutes. And if that passenger didn't actually want anything and was just waiting for the lavatory, they just couldn't help but make idle conversation usually starting with, "That looks good, what is it?"

Certain flight attendants preferred to work certain positions on the aircraft because it better suited their personalities. For example, someone who was well organized would enjoy working in the galley. Some took this position a little too seriously, however, and became the galley tyrant. There lay an imaginary line between the galley and the aisles, and if you crossed that line, the galley tyrant would blast you with their death stare. Personally, if I had to work in the galley, I preferred the you-know-where-it-is-get-it-yourself approach. Working in the galley also meant being willing to lift heavy items, get dirty, get burnt, and maybe chip a nail or two. I used to enjoy working in the galley when it only entailed galley work. Once the galley position also had to work the aisle, I found it to be too demanding.

Those who preferred working the aisles with the passengers tended to be more social, or at least really good actors. Or, like myself, no longer wished to work the galley position and didn't have any other suitable option. The club class position was where you would find flight attendants who knew how to dote on passengers, were highly organized, and didn't mind working alone or serving the cockpit.

In over twenty years as a flight attendant, I've only had to work club a total of three times. All these times were not by choice. The flight positions for your workday were chosen strictly by seniority. Given a choice, I would always work in the economy section, specifically as aft as possible. I guess I felt more at ease, since I wasn't comfortable doting on people. It was not something we did in my household. We were more of a fend-for-yourself family. Eat or get eaten.

Survival-of-the-fittest-Darwinism-type household. In fact, if you really wanted to save something to eat, you'd better label it with your name or else it's considered fair game. If no one volunteered to work club class and I was the most junior in seniority and no one would accept my bribe, then I was left with no choice.

The first time I ever had to work club class was because no one liked the flight director and working this class at that time meant working alongside the flight director for most of the day. It was awful. I hated my colleagues that day. The flight director had me tend to all the passengers on my own while she read her newspaper and shared all her woe-is-me stories. If she were my kid, she would have gotten a "suck it up" response, but instead I bit my tongue and tried to smile sympathetically.

My second experience working club happened on a turnaround (a.k.a. turn)* because no one wanted to do all that extra service in such a short amount of flight time. The bad news was that I couldn't get the darn wine bottles opened. The good news was that it was, in fact, a truly short flight, and my flight director had been super helpful.

My third and final time working club class was very odd. It was completely unexpected because there were crew members operating that flight who I knew enjoyed working that section. Not to mention, the flight director was quite personable, and the flight was a long overseas one. And yet, there I was.

I wasn't even going to work that flight in the first place, but my brother and sister-in-law were travelling on it and had asked if I could request it. I managed to hold enough seniority to get awarded the flight but only as the most junior flight attendant. After failing to persuade anyone in the crew to swap positions, I pulled out my club class for dummies cheat sheets from my crew bag to help me figure out what to do. Services on board could change dramatically from year to year, so even though I had worked club two other times, years had passed in between. Unfortunately, my service sheets were just as old. Looks like I was going to have to wing it. (See what I did there? Wing it?)

This proved to be challenging, however, because I never personally had the privilege of sitting in this section as a passenger, not even when deadheading*, so I didn't know what the service should look like. Sure, I had watched the how-to videos and read the memos from the company, but I had never really paid too much attention to them since my chances of working club were usually slim. My outdated service cheat sheets were mocking me and so was my flight director. I chose not to take it personally when she laughed at me and my archaic services. I soon found myself giving a self-pep talk, *How hard could this be? What do club class passengers expect? To be waited on and get free stuff. Easy. You've got this.* With the fake confidence I had learned over the years, I managed to serve everyone their meals and drinks without a hitch. I was feeling rather good about myself. One of my passengers, in fact, approached me on her way to the lavatories to comment on what wonderful service she had been receiving. This was her first time sitting in club class and said she would absolutely do it again. I wanted to let her know she probably *wouldn't* receive this same service again if I wasn't her flight attendant, since I had basically made it up as I went along, but hey, why pop her bubble? I felt like a superstar employee. Then one of my colleagues working economy came to visit me and asked if I managed all right with the specialty coffees. *Wait, what? They get specialty coffees?* My dumfounded look answered her question.

Another distinction between flight attendants was in the distance of their commute. Some lived locally in their permanent home, others lived in crash pads,* and others lived not only out-of-city or province but also out-of-country. I always admired the commitment required of these latter flight attendants. Regardless of where a flight attendant had to commute from, there was no tolerance for lateness, and as such, flight attendants became self-taught power walkers (many in heels). You can usually tell when a flight attendant is walking behind you because of the fast stomping of their heels and the speeding sound of rolling luggage.

Even though the physical and emotional characteristics of flight attendants had changed greatly over the years, the smile remained. No matter which positions flight attendants were working or which type of animal their personality represented, the smile forever remained a mystery. Whether called a flight attendant, trolley dolly, sky waiter or waitress, steward or stewardess, air host or hostess—or my husband's favourite—a short-skirted sky slut, I was proud to have been part of a flight crew.

. . .

*crash pad: Not as in a foam pad used for protection from falls, but rather this is a house or apartment shared with multiple flight crew usually close to the airport and usually temporary. Some may house just flight attendants or just pilots and some only men or women.

*deadheading: Not as in the Grateful Dead fans or zombies or even when dead flower heads are removed from a plant, but rather crew members who are travelling as passengers on the company's time to work from a different city. They may not necessarily be in uniform (incognito deadheading is preferable).

*shadow flight: A flight in which new hires follow the other flight attendants without having any real responsibilities and are supervised by the flight director, like a trial run before the real deal.

*turnaround (a.k.a. turn): Not as in to move in a circular motion, but rather this is a flight that leaves and returns back the same day.

Chapter Two

The Job

You know those commercials advertising the latest, most amazing new drug that will be life-altering but also come with a slew of possible side effects? The job of a flight attendant was that drug. The list of "side effects" consisted of a higher chance of cancer, exposure to radiation and diseases or infections, and sleep disorders or deprivation resulting in extreme fatigue, just to name a few. All this and yet, being a flight attendant was still looked upon as being one of the most desirable professions. Some associated being a flight attendant with glamour, elegance, and confidence, while others saw it as a means to free flights. Let me shed some light on this.

The job of a flight attendant was far more than just showing up in uniform serving some meals and drinks to passengers and laying over in different cities around the world. Until you've stepped foot in a flight attendant's sensible, flat galley shoe, you couldn't genuinely appreciate just how unglamorous and unappreciative of a job it was. I've had to deal with (or witnessed colleagues who had to deal with) many "side effects" as a flight attendant, but these were the common ones: physical pain, odours, flatulence, sleep deprivation, illness and injuries, survival on protein bars and dehydration, emotional stress, flexibility, and loneliness.

Even though they may serve you drinks, flight attendants were essentially trained to save lives in case of an emergency. As much as many passengers may think differently, their job did not include stowing oversized and overweight luggage in the overhead bin. I would assist in lifting bags or finding room for them, but unless the passenger was elderly or physically disabled, the rule was that if they packed it, they lifted it. The muscle strain on my lower back was plentiful without the additional lifting of others' luggage. Lifting heavy canisters in the galleys; having to store and remove service items in and out of the overhead bins; pushing and pulling heavy service trolleys; constantly raising, lowering, and body twisting to perform passenger services in the aisles; and the opening and closing of the heavy aircraft doors all put enough pressure on the back.

In addition to the work strains on the back, the long stretches of time while standing and the changes in air pressure could sometimes cause uncomfortable swelling in the feet and ankles as well as sore legs. I always knew when I had been off work for too long because after my first flight back my legs would feel incredibly tired, sore, and heavy. Eventually most flight attendants ended up trading in their fashionable socks or stockings for compression wear. Despite the assistance from these in pushing the blood back up from the feet to the heart, flight crew were still susceptible to ugly spider and varicose veins. If only the sheer ugliness of my veins could have been enough to deter angry passengers from throwing insults my way, I would have embraced them.

Another unfortunate side effect of being a flight attendant was learning to become nose-blind to *all* the smells that came with the job, which was easier said than done unfortunately. We always knew when someone was applying nail polish because the strong smell would permeate through the entire aircraft. The same was true when my company thought it was a good idea to serve chicken curry. (This meal option was soon eliminated after numerous complaints.) By the end of a flight, the uniform that others might have perceived as elegant and glamorous would reek of all the unpleasant smells that a plane had to offer. It was usually a mix of spilled something or other (with my luck it tended to be tomato juice), a waft of urine that always seemed to linger when anywhere near the lavs, gas smells that managed to trap themselves into our fire-retardant woolen uniforms, and a splash of vomit. If I was coming home from work, my family knew not to approach me until after I had the chance to shower and decontaminate.

When applying to be a flight attendant, nobody ever told you about flatulence. Trapped gas was a quite common ailment associated with flying. When on the plane for so many hours, it got trapped and accumulated in the stomach causing it to swell like a balloon. Passing gas (a.k.a. breaking wind, farting, tooting, letting one rip, cutting the cheese) was the only solution. Even though it was a common and natural occurrence, I still preferred that passengers and crew refrained from crop dusting.* If possible, saving it for the privacy of the lavatories or even the car ride home would have been much appreciated. I was engulfed by a fellow passenger's eau-de-stank aroma when I had the pleasure of sitting behind him on a ten-hour flight once. Every hour on the hour he'd release his stink bomb. As much as I made a lot of fuss over his odour with my "that's disgusting!" or "you've got to be kidding me" remarks, it never fazed my gracious passenger to stop. Of course, no one I was travelling with would switch seats with me either.

Sometimes passengers and crew would be able to blame the stink on others because there were always so many people in close quarters, which made it difficult to pinpoint the guilty. This was not the case in the cockpit, however. I happened to be getting something in the forward galley one day, and while I was there, the flight director asked if I wouldn't mind bringing a coffee into the cockpit for the captain. When I entered, I found the first officer wearing his oxygen mask and the captain laughing hysterically. I stood in the doorway unsure of what was happening or if he still wanted his coffee. The first officer cautiously removed his mask and asked me if I smelt anything. The captain had apparently let one rip so violently that the first officer felt the need to don his mask. Luckily, it had already dissipated by the time I had opened the door. My look had changed from confused to disgusted to relieved, all in a matter of seconds. I handed the captain his coffee in hopes he wouldn't release another one while I was still there and then dashed out. If you were one of the lucky few who was successfully able to build up a smell intolerance and become nose-blind, you held a truly special power.

Unfortunately, no one held the power to function without sleep. Even a cyborg with its enhanced capabilities still needed to be recharged for peak performance. Flying at all times of the day and night sometimes made the necessity for proper sleep challenging for flight attendants. When I had a family with small children and a dog to care for, naps were not something I could easily squeeze in before having to work throughout the night. Like many of my colleagues, I was tired before the workday had even started. Being sleep deprived coupled with the effects of jet lag resulted in a less-than-ideal state, and yet flight crew were still expected to be alert and ready in case of an emergency. I will not go into depth on the issues pertaining to lack of sleep since there is a full chapter dedicated to tiredness, but I will say that fatigue is an all-too-common symptom, so if you see a flight attendant trying to catch a little shut-eye during a break, please don't poke him or her awake but rather call on one of the others. If you find you are the only one awake, and the entire cabin has fallen asleep because there's an air leak and you somehow escaped the effects of hypoxia, good luck.

With the amount of radiation, germs, illnesses, and dangers circling around in an aircraft, it's no wonder flight attendants weren't in full hazmat suits. Having to work in restricted spaces for long periods of time meant germs were a sizable concern. I made sure to practice good hygiene through frequent handwashing and being aware of those who were potentially sick. Over the years I have seen my fair share of diseases and viruses.

Influenza, commonly known as the flu, was probably the most common viral infection, but not the most concerning since people were still permitted to travel and knew how to manage it. The concerning title was reserved for hand, foot, and mouth disease - a common viral infection in young children. If still in the contagious stage, they were obviously not allowed to travel back home. Not wanting to be left behind, many parents would attempt to conceal their sick child in a blanket, and if they only got discovered once in flight, madness would spew. Other parents with small children would be particularly upset and rightfully so. The guilty parents would be defensive and upset from all the stresses. The cabin crew would be left trying to keep everyone calm while the pilots would have to relay all the information to the ground before arrival. Our technique of physically lowering ourselves to the seated passenger's level to appear non-menacing and sympathetic would be well practiced. Sometimes just listening and being sympathetic was all that was required in reassuring a passenger, such as when passengers would see what they thought was smoke coming out of the plane before landing, and I'd have to reassure them that it was not smoke but rather fuel dumping.*

Sometimes, when waiting to board, I would find myself unknowingly humming the circus theme song. I guess subconsciously I must have been anticipating an entertaining show. It wasn't until a colleague pointed this out to me that I even realized I was doing it. Inevitably, germs and bodily matter were part of each "show" and flight attendants had no choice but to deal with them. We used to provide a complimentary blanket to anyone who requested one and then we would collect them at the end of the flight. If this wasn't bad enough, we had to fold and store them. Besides some food or drink remnants, many came back with dandruff or skin flakes. Some blankets we purposely left with the passengers because we knew what had happened under that blanket and wanted no part of it. As I found out, the mile-high club wasn't reserved solely for the lavatories. At the end of one of my flights, I remember walking down the aisles collecting blankets in preparation for our descent when I had witnessed a passenger in her twenties straddling her male companion in his seat, covered by one of our blankets. The disgusting image had burned my eyeballs, so I had just kept walking and pretended I didn't see a thing. After the SARS outbreak of 2003, all blankets had to be individually sealed and once used, no longer returned to the flight attendant.

Having a thick skin meant more to a flight attendant than being able to handle criticism and being easily offended. It meant literally having thick, impenetrable skin that could resist pain. I've seen many colleagues show up to work slightly sick or injured because either they had already checked in,* or booking off* just wasn't worth using their hard-earned sick credits.* I ended up going to work even with a nasty burn on my arm when I was pulling a meal out of the oven. My then two-year-old son decided he would come up from behind me and try to reach in to help, and as I bum scooched him out of harm's way, I managed to scorch my upper arm on the hot oven rack. I applied some burn cream and left for work with some missing skin.

The physical demands of being on the job also included knowing how to deal with hunger and when to squeeze in a meal. Being able to survive on protein bars was essential when working as a flight attendant. Many times, flight crew just didn't have time to eat a proper meal during the flight but couldn't afford to pass out from starvation. They needed that boost of energy that a quick protein bar could provide. Unless of course it contained peanuts and there was someone on board with a peanut allergy, in which case you'd have to tuck it away and search for other suitable options.

As much as even flight crew were entitled to breaks, many times these were just not feasible. You had to eat what you could when you could. If you were waiting for your scheduled break time, you could be left not having eaten anything at all. Eating while everyone else was still out in the aisles working, however, was extremely risky and could lead to a brawl, so you had to either be careful with your timing or be very discreet. If other hungry flight attendants saw you eating while they were still working, this could get real ugly.

Besides eating properly, drinking plenty of water was crucial while flying. Air was much drier at high altitudes, and so staying hydrated required drinking eight to ten ounces of water for roughly every one hour of flight. I always knew when I wasn't drinking enough water while working because I would end up getting headaches. Not getting enough water could not only result in headaches but also fatigue, a dry mouth, and nausea. At the beginning of my flights, my colleagues and I would each take claim to one 1.5 litre bottle of water to drink from for the duration of the day. Some flights may have required more and some less, but it was a good gauge as to how much we were drinking.

Being emotionally strong is important when getting hit in all directions from various stressors particularly coming from passengers. Stresses related to the flight, such as weather issues, turbulence, and possible emergency situations, including medicals, were nothing compared to the rude and obnoxious behaviour of disruptive passengers. They could be threatening, abusive, and insulting, and since flight attendants couldn't exactly run away or call for immediate backup, they were at their mercy. The saving grace was the satisfaction in knowing that once landed your disruptive passenger would be getting interrogated by the authorities while you'd be off the plane enjoying the rest of your day.

But emotional stress that flight attendants dealt with wasn't limited to the passengers. If you were the type of person who did not like change and preferred to stick to a regimented schedule, being a flight attendant might not be for you. There was no choice but to be flexible with this job. Changes were constant with an airline. Mechanical issues; weather; airport incidents, such as baggage, security, and strikes; as well as disasters and pandemics could all play a part on whether you worked your scheduled flight or not.

I was required to work a minimum of sixty-five flight hours a month up to a maximum of ninety-five hours. We were on duty* from showtime* to release time;* however, we were paid from the time the wheel chock blocks were removed from behind the plane's tires allowing it to push back to the time those blocks were placed back on. (We called this flight time block-to-block.) Therefore, when flight attendants were quickly trying to get everyone seated and ready for take-off, it was because their time clock had still not started. Regardless of whether a flight attendant was on reserve or on a schedule, nothing was ever consistent. Schedules could change at the last minute, aircraft could get swapped out, or weather issues could come into play. Things in the airline business tended to have a snowball effect. So, for example, if there was a mechanical issue with a plane overseas and now they needed a replacement plane but by the time that replacement plane arrived the crew was no longer legal (permitted to work the flight according to union rules), they'd have to use a different crew from a nearby route which *was* legal. But then their spots needed to be filled and so on and so on, until all the king's horses and all the king's men *could* put Humpty Dumpty back together again.

The flexibility requirements of the job meant the possibility of having to accept a draft.* Even my days off from work were not untouchable to the airline. The only thing was they had to get a hold of me first. My family was trained to always say I wasn't home if they answered a call from the airline; however, on one of my days off, I accidentally answered the phone and couldn't come up with a decent lie on the spot. Acceptable lies included you were drinking (even if it was breakfast time), there was no babysitter available, it was the wrong person (in which you'd then pretend to be someone else), or even that all your uniform pieces were at the drycleaners because your house was sprayed by a skunk. Not acceptable excuses included no transportation available (they'd call you a cab), no dog sitter available (fur babies didn't count), or you were high (you'd get fired).

One time getting drafted worked in my favour, however. I had just arrived at the airport on the way to my flight when crew sked* called me. Thinking it might have been about my flight, I answered it and was drafted onto a different flight instead. The aircraft was already prepared to leave except they were missing one flight attendant. I made my way over to the new gate and because the flight director knew me and I was the most senior on the crew, he saved my preferred position for me. Not only that, but my checks had already been completed, and the passengers and cabin were all secured to depart. My new turn landed back home around the same time as my original flight except I was paid more for being drafted and having a slightly longer flight time.

The draft didn't always work in my favour, however. When I was the most junior on a layover and therefore had no option, I was drafted from my lovely two-day layover with my crew to now travel elsewhere as a times-one and return home a whole day later. Being a times-one was never fun. This meant having to join other crews as the extra wherever I was needed but usually entailed travelling by myself in between the flights. The transport and hotel reservations always seemed to be an issue too.

As inconsistent as my schedule might have been, the good news was that because it was so flexible, it offered me the opportunity to build my schedule according to my needs, dependent on seniority of course. If I wanted to go on a school field trip with my daughter, for instance, I could. In fact, many of the parents at my kids' school didn't even know I had a job because I was always around. When my children were little, my husband and I chose to not put them in daycare or hire a babysitter (some may call this practice masochistic), and so I would typically leave for work Friday evenings (to the tears of my middle child) and return on the Sunday, while my husband would work every day Monday through Friday. My other two children didn't seem to mind when I left for work, but god forbid when their daddy would have to leave on a business trip. It was like someone had died with the number of tears and wailing happening. I'd have to throw on a funny movie just to distract them so they could settle down.

As much as this schedule involved sacrificing some weekend family time, it worked for us. It was thanks to my job that my husband was able to appreciate all that raising children entailed. He never took the role of a parent for granted, and the kids got to experience fun daddy time until mean mommy had to straighten them out again every Monday. Once the children became older and more self-sufficient, I was able to shift my schedule so that I would work during the week and enjoy weekends with the family (when I wanted to).

This brought us to the aspect of being lonely as a flight attendant. As much as we were always around people, those people were not the same as being with family and close friends. Aside from the obvious of missing my family, I also missed my dog and sleeping in my bed. I even missed Fred (a.k.a. Furry Red Evil Demon), the tiny red squirrel that claimed himself as the ruler of my backyard and chased all the other critters away. It was also not uncommon for a flight attendant to miss important events, holidays, or family functions. I missed the birth of my godchild while I was operating a flight and then ended up speeding down the highway just so I could get to visiting hours on time at the hospital. Unfortunately, I didn't miss my daughter's first sentence, in which she said, "piece of shit," and then had to take the blame. To be fair, I *was* assembling a piece of crappy furniture when she decided she would mimic me. Strangely enough my husband had the trucker mouth, and yet I was to blame for my daughter's choice in her first sentence.

Sometimes, however, having to leave the country would work in my favour. If I really didn't want to attend someone's party but felt bad saying no, I could just use the work excuse. After we had children, we never accepted an invitation in which they were not allowed (I'm starting to think we *were* masochists) and so attending a party meant more work, unless it was a special occasion in which going to work was worth it, as in, "Sorry, I have to go to work."

In the days before I had children, having to go to work after a party would prove challenging. I remember partying with friends for New Year's Eve and then having to quietly step over sleeping bodies so I could be at work by the crack of dawn. I felt like someone trying to avoid setting off a laser security system, as I not only had to watch for limbs but also scattered beer bottles and half-eaten food remnants. Being a flight attendant also meant being aware that even when not in uniform, humiliating acts (including intoxication) reflected poorly on the company and could lead to dismissal (particularly if still on the probationary six-month period). Luckily for me my party days of throwing up with my head out the side of a car travelling one hundred kilometres per hour were behind me.

During times of loneliness and homesickness the galley could always be counted on to be a great distraction and even quite therapeutic. There were no conversation boundaries when on an aircraft and nothing was held back among the crew. Behind the galley curtain was where all the "tea was spilled," and sex topics were openly discussed. Recipe exchanging, singing, playing games, doing makeovers, and discussing other tamer topics also occurred but weren't as stimulating. It was always kind of weird, though, how after sharing all our deepest thoughts with one another, the moment we stepped foot off the plane it was "bye!" and we might not have seen each other again for years. Once home, it was my time to unwind and recount the crazies of the day with my family. Hopefully, this would be over some chocolates gifted by a passenger (by the way, flight attendants like gifts).

In essence being a flight attendant meant being a superhero. They had to be strong; be immune to things that could stop others, such as smells, germs, and injuries; not require a lot of sleep or food; handle constant change and being a loner; be comfortable flying (even Wonder Woman had the assistance of her invisible jet); be required to save people every now and then; and act (even if questionable at times). The difference was that flight attendants could do all this and much more while dressed in far better attire.

***booking off:** The term used for when flight crew call in sick and therefore cannot fly. They will need to book back on to return to flying.

*checked in: This is a confirmation of your presence on a flight. It has to be done within a certain time period.

*crew sked: This is short for crew scheduling and is a group of people who flight crew rely on for anything pertaining to their flight schedule.

*crop dusting: Not as in spraying crops with a fertilizer from an aircraft, but rather this is the act of walking down the aisle of a passenger plane while passing wind through the cabin. This performance should ideally start from the opposite end of where you'll be working.

*draft: Not as in the beer or the first version of a manuscript, but rather this is when flight attendants are called by crew sked to operate a flight not on their schedule. If they do not answer the call, they cannot get drafted (unless they are out of base and then they have no choice because they are technically still on duty). If they do answer the call but are not legal, they can also not be drafted (hence all the number of drinkers in the company at all times of the day).

*duty: Not to be confused with doody or poop, this is a period of time in which flight crew belong to the company as opposed to off-duty, which is more of a catch-me-if-you-can situation.

*fuel dumping: This occurs when an aircraft has to release fuel in order to safely land or take-off due to weight issues. Although this is not a frequent occurrence, it is normal if a flight has to land before it is planned, since not all aircraft are capable of this and therefore might just have to circle before landing instead.

*release time: Not as in the appropriate time to relieve one's flatulence, but rather this is the time flight crew are no longer on duty (usually fifteen minutes after the chock blocks are placed back on).

*showtime: Not as in just before the start of a play, but rather this is the scheduled time flight attendants are required to show up at a specified location (usually on the aircraft) before a flight.

*sick credits: These are like points earned from working, and the reward is being able to still get paid even if you need to call in sick. Every credit is equal to one flight hour, so for example, if the flight you are scheduled to work is worth five hours, you would use five sick credits (easier said than done as the most credits you can earn monthly is four). If flight crew *predicted* a sickness coming on and weren't able to donate their scheduled flight to someone else, they would at least attempt to switch it to a flight worth fewer hours so that fewer sick credits would be used. Empty sick banks are common.

Chapter Three

The Balance

To successfully last as a flight attendant, they had to learn how to balance life on the ground with life in the air. Many of my colleagues excelled at this and held other jobs, such as teachers, nurses, therapists, designers, and so on. I found that either they embraced this and even managed to juggle multiple jobs and a family, or they would end up calling it quits and hanging up their wings within a few months. If they did stick around long enough, they would discover just how unique and adventurous (a.k.a. crazy) every flight could be. A flight attendant could return home comfortably knowing that once they were off that plane, only memories of the day would follow. Correction, memories and odours.

The degree of difficulty in balancing life lay in seniority. This was determined by your hire date and was key in an airline. It was the difference between being on reserve, working all the holidays, and getting stuck with all the crappy routes that no one wanted, or choosing when and where you wanted to work and lying on the beach for weeks at a time. The number of hires who proceeded you would determine how quickly you could scale that seniority list.

When I was first hired, I, too, started on reserve. This basically meant crew sked could call me all day and any day that wasn't my scheduled day off and send me anywhere they desired—all in a matter of under three hours. (This was later revised strictly to either a.m. or p.m. reserve groupings.) My time on reserve was before cell phones became popular, so instead, I had a pager. This was great for when someone was looking for you, but then you had to go on the hunt for a pay phone and hopefully you had a quarter handy. Luckily, my reserve life was short-lived. I had built up enough seniority to acquire a schedule.

Schedules were allotted by seniority of course so requesting to work a certain day or flight was not guaranteed. The most you could hope for when requesting a schedule as a junior flight attendant was your selected days off, but not if it was a holiday—let's keep it real. Because flight attendants' schedules could vary so dramatically from one another and changes occurred frequently, it was always difficult to make plans with co-workers when not flying.

I was part of a running group at my company but trying to coordinate races together proved quite challenging. I participated in a few of the running events; however, when the group leader left the airline, no one else (including myself) was willing to take on the frustrating task of organizing races where only a handful of people would end up showing. Like when a colleague from my initial training class used to attempt anniversary get togethers for our class, but dates and locations would keep having to get changed to accommodate schedules and then only a few would show up anyway.

Working with people you knew was also not guaranteed. Years would pass before you'd see certain familiar faces. It wasn't uncommon for someone to ask me, "How many children do you have now?" or "You still work here?" This always made it fun, however, when you'd finally meet up with someone you really enjoyed working with but hadn't seen in a while. My one colleague and I had a mutual friend outside of the company and when we had the opportunity to work together on a long overseas flight to Rome, we thought it would be fun to "bring" her along. We put a picture of our friend's face on my phone and propped it up on our beverage trolley as we served the passengers together. The passengers who noticed this found it amusing but most were half asleep, so it didn't even faze them when we'd ask our phone friend to not be so lazy and start helping. We even let her rest in the designated crew seats (not that she deserved it) all while wearing the uniform scarf by tying it around the bottom of the phone. We flipped through magazine photos together and even fed her cherry tomatoes when we thought she looked hungry. We used my friend's phone to take pictures of the three of us so we could show our honorary flight attendant once we returned. She thought it was hilarious and appreciated the effort.

As you can see just trying to keep your airline life in order was difficult enough without introducing home life. Everyone had her own obligations and responsibilities outside of work (some more than others), but what I found extremely beneficial were calendars and lists. I still do. They were the yin to my yang. They added normal to my crazy. They were why my family teased me, but I didn't care (I still don't).

When I would get my work schedule for the month, the first thing I did was add it to my calendar, which was already filled in with all the other scheduled appointments and activities. If anything overlapped, it was time to start making some changes. Before having children, the calendar would predominantly be filled with flights. When my children were little, the calendar was already packed with all their various activities, school events, parties, and appointments before I even started filling in my flights, and as they became older and more self-sufficient, the calendar would start looking much less cluttered.

As my life status shifted over the years in the airline industry, my work schedule shifted accordingly. When I was single, I could fly wherever and whenever I chose to, since I had no one to be accountable to. This worked out well because I was on reserve at first and then when I did hold a schedule, I still couldn't afford to be picky as a junior flight attendant. When I got married, I had to consider my husband's needs; although he never minded when I'd leave for the weekend so he could get in some bro-time (or bachelor time as he would call it). When I became a mother with small children, I worked weekends. And as a mom with older kids, I worked weekdays.

I never felt guilty being a working mom and having to leave for a couple days because the way I saw it, this made me a better mom. Let me explain. When I worked weekends, I was full-on there for everyone, Monday through Friday. I brought the kids to and from school, helped with homework, attended every school or extra-curricular activity, cooked, cleaned, and did every other regular "mom or wife thing." By Friday night, I was usually spent and would need some alone time to recharge, which worked out great because I could go to work, fly overnight, stay in a hotel, and be back on Sunday as fresh mommy. The kids fared well, too, because daddy was the fun guy, so on weekends the kids didn't have to bother with boring homework or making beds. Because most parties happened on weekends, this was also a win-win. My hubby enjoyed them; I did not. I never stayed away longer than two nights at a time, so it wasn't like I missed out on watching the kids grow. I always made sure they had everything they needed before I would leave for work, such as food and the to-do list, and my husband would make sure the house was still standing and the kids were still alive for when I returned.

When the kids were older and more self-sufficient, my job became ever more ideal because I could now work during the week and enjoy weekends off with my husband (and kids when they weren't avoiding their now not-so-cool-anymore parents). I could build my schedule around school events and functions and even attend the odd party. The flexibility in my job allowed me the freedom to choose what kind of a mother and wife I wanted to be and whether to work shorter flights or fly away for days at a time. When the kids became old enough, they were even able to join me for little weekend getaways. They could go back to school on Monday and when asked what they did on the weekend, they could answer, "Oh, I was just in Venice." Spoiled? Yes.

I dedicated five years into creating my little travelling family, which meant I was off from flying quite a lot during that period. Within those years, I was pregnant a total of five times. I carried three babies to full term (or close to) and lost two after my first pregnancy. I was placed on disability with my first and fourth pregnancies and took a short leave after my two miscarriages. During my first pregnancy, my right kidney had become blocked, and I needed a nephrostomy tube placed through my back and into my kidney to drain my urine. The doctors thought it was kidney stones, but it turned out to simply be the pressure from my womb. For four months, attached to my pants, was a bag and tube contraption holding my urine. It was safe to say that I didn't get any of those professional maternity shots taken where the mom-to-be looked perfectly blissful. On a positive note, the tube not only allowed me to use the bathroom half the amount I normally would, but I could also write my name in the snow (I never did). Because of this contraption and the fact that I was on heavy-duty pain medication, I never ended up flying during that pregnancy. I was also kept from flying for the following pregnancies due to the possibility it could happen again, but I eventually returned when I was pregnant with my last. (I might have begged them by this point.) Returning to work after my experiences almost felt like an odd reward for my sacrifices, but it was my little me time, in which even the crazies were welcomed.

If I could maintain some sort of organization at home, all was good. Once my calendar was all in order, I could concentrate on my never-ending lists. I had lists for everything. I had a shopping list, my to-do list, my husband's to-do list, the kids' to-do list, the activities list, the how-to-care-for-my-dog-when-I-was-away list, the things-I-wanted-to-see-and-do list, the books-to-read list, and finally the movies-to-watch list. I even kept a mental list of things I needed to check before leaving the house, such as making sure the lights were off, the doors were locked, and the dog's blanket was fluffed exactly right (yes, he's spoiled).

Before leaving for a flight, I would leave my husband a detailed list of what to do while I was gone divided up into days. Not because I didn't believe he could get things done, but because both he and I knew just how forgetful he could be. This included everything from reminding him to feed the dog to not buying yet *another* couch while I was away. Sometimes it was more of a what-*not*-to-do list.

To be fair, my husband had always been very forgetful, to the point where if I asked him to pick up two items while he was out, I was lucky if he came back with one. He's the kind of guy who would walk into a room and ask, "Why am I here again?" Perhaps we could have used those red flight tags all around my house as reminders to close doors and cupboards and turn off lights and televisions. And as for the couch reference above, he had the habit of unnecessarily buying couches and televisions. He also once purchased a new minivan while I was away, and another time, I opened the garage to park my car after coming home from a flight only to find the toilet from my bathroom there.

Besides the lists, I would always leave all my flight and hotel information, just in case something was to happen. As geeky as all my lists, notes, and planning might have been, they kept our chaotic lives somewhat organized and manageable.

When the kids were still little and it looked like I had figured out how to keep my work and home life pretty balanced, the world decided to throw a wrench named type 1 diabetes* into our lives. When my son was diagnosed with this at the age of three, just the thought of leaving for work became incredibly stressful. Even though diabetes was manageable, it could be extremely unpredictable and did not allow for breaks. One minute everything seemed fine, and then suddenly his life could be in danger. Once I was in the air there was no more contact with home. If something were to happen while I was away, I couldn't just pack up and leave. Overtime I learned to relax and trust that he was in good hands and would be well taken care of. Work even proved to serve as a distraction from the worrying. Initially, my manager had given me some time off work so my husband and I could learn how to manage my son's disease, but then once I returned, we had to learn how to add diabetes into our work-and-life equation.

We had our share of challenges, including many "highs" and "lows" (common diabetes lingo), but soon enough it became part of our norm and life continued as usual. With the exception that now we carried a diabetes bag around, poked our son's fingers multiple times a day, injected him with needles, weighed and counted all his carbs, and would casually ask him if he was "high." Luckily, nothing out of the norm ever happened while I was away. My son made sure to save his highs—vomiting, bedwetting, and nosebleeds—and his extreme lows—passing out and trips to the hospital—for when I was present.

Aside from having to balance my personal life with my flying career, there were also work stages that I went through which found their place accordingly. Stage one was exciting. I'd be at the aircraft well before showtime and well prepared. My uniform would be in perfect condition. Hair, makeup, nails—all pristine. I was smiling. I was pumped. I was ready. During this stage I *wanted* to talk to the passengers, wear my high heels, and quickly answer call lights. I was a shining employee radiating rainbows and lollipops. This stage correlated with my pre-baby life, so finding a balance was fairly simple, and my lists mainly consisted of what purchases I needed to make.

Fast forward a few years, and we had stage two. Now I had settled in and realized that not everyone was so nice, and sleep was much more important. I emphasize sleep because this was also the stage in which I now had three small children. The balancing act became a little trickier, and the lists began to flourish. I would get to the airport with enough time to grab the essential coffee before going on the aircraft in my uniform, which looked decent enough but could probably use a little ironing. Hair, makeup, and nails were satisfactory. I was still smiling but just not all the time now. If I was smiling when in front of the passengers, that was good enough. I had arrived. I was ready to get the flight done.

In this stage, I would engage in conversation with the passengers if they started it first, focusing primarily on my section. I would switch my high heels to galley shoes* immediately once in the air. The call lights would hopefully get passed on to the newbie flight attendants who were still in stage one and therefore more than happy to leave their radiating energy down the aisles. Sarcasm became very prominent in this stage. I remember working with a flight attendant who was clearly deep in this stage of their career, and during our pre-flight briefing,* he demonstrated it quite vividly. The crew was all seated in the club class section of the aircraft, and as per the norm, we were waiting for our pilots to start the briefing. Typically, when at an English-speaking home base,* the briefing was conducted in English. Made sense. On this day, our pilot decided he would start the meeting in French. My colleague frantically started pressing his number-one button on his armrest asking if it was broken. I wanted to laugh so badly but had to contain myself and ended up giving a little snort instead. Along with the volume control on the passenger armrests was the channel selector. The number one was for English, and the number two was for French.

The third and final stage in my flying career was coming to terms with the realization that I was indeed a lifer. This was the stage in which I had to balance living with teenagers, a husband, and a dog. The lists were starting to grow lists of their own, taking on their own lives because they had become so vast. In this stage, I no longer had a job; I had a career. If I ever left my career as a flight attendant, I could become a professional list maker. Everything became strategic.

I could now roll out of bed and be ready to leave the house in as little as fifteen minutes flat. My uniform was deemed fine if it could pass the sniff test. My hair became a tousled look above the collar line, which was my excuse for not brushing or styling it, makeup became unnecessary, and my nails were now kept purposely short. I would arrive at my briefing still with a coffee in hand and still early. Arriving early was not because I was a keener but rather because the lineup for coffee was unpredictable, and I needed my java fix. Talking to the passengers became more of a nod of acknowledgement. My heels were traded in for sensible but still legal (permitted by uniform rules) flats. *What call light? I didn't hear anything.*

Regardless of which stage I was in, my lists remained the constant to keep life in balance. They were my go-to, my rock, my sanity. I even had a list on what I was looking for in a partner after I had dumped my ex, but my husband threw it out when we first started dating. The more responsibilities I had, whether they were my spouse, my kids, my pets, or any other jobs, the more organized I needed to be to remain sane. My lists were my form of organized chaos so that I could maintain the balance required in being a flight attendant as well as a wife and a mother, without going completely insane.

*galley shoes: These are the flat and usually very well-worn-in shoes in which flight attendants are permitted to wear during their in-flight services.

*home base: Not as in going all the way with your partner, but rather this is the city where your trips start and end. You may not necessarily live at your home base, but your schedules are built around this.

*pre-flight briefing: A crew briefing in which the captain and flight director provide information regarding the flight as well as review certain procedures.

*type 1 diabetes: This non-preventable autoimmune disease, in which the pancreas stops producing insulin, is the most severe form of diabetes, striking children and adults suddenly, leaving them dependent on injected or pumped insulin for life.

Chapter Four

The Training

After a month of extensive initial training when first hired, I had to further endure a day of pure agony, as flight crew are subjected to recurrent annual training and exams. This was exacerbated when my first aid and CPR training were also up for renewal every other year. As much as I had dreaded this day, I knew it was unavoidable, as failure to complete and pass meant saying goodbye to my flying career.

I always made sure to double check my training dates every year. This became especially important after an incident I had heard during galley talk. A colleague of mine accidentally went to class on the wrong date. He sat down and since the class hadn't started yet, he engaged in small talk with some of the other flight attendants. He thought it was a little odd that he didn't know anyone, but he chalked it up to a room full of new hires, since our airline had recently gone through a big hiring stage. The instructor began the class, and that's when my colleague noticed the welcome sign from a *different* airline—one which shared the same training facility with us. He apologized to the group and left but not before being invited to stay and join them anyway.

Making sure I showed up at the correct time was equally important as the correct day. I was in class one year, and we were a few hours into our day when another colleague walked in all eager and ready to start. That year the company thought it was a good idea to distribute our training schedule in Zulu time,* but it seemed not everyone got the memo. My confused colleague was permitted to reschedule his annual for another day, and my company reverted to local times for training after that year. One year, I barely made it to class in time due to construction on the highway. When I dashed into the room all panic-stricken, the instructor looked up from behind the desk and said, "Don't worry, you made it by twenty seconds." I felt so extremely relieved, but the stress of the drive caused me to give myself an extra hour's time every year after that experience.

The annual training day was intended to review and test our skills and knowledge, pertaining primarily to emergency situations. One of the requirements was to use what we had been taught to effectively execute an emergency in the simulator. This involved splitting up the class in half so that half would act as the passengers while the rest were the active crew members, and then we'd swap for the next scenario. Some flight attendants were like natural born actors, and we'd have no problem understanding what they were trying to portray. Others, like me, were not so convincing, so I'd end up saying, "I am now checking the door for heat," for instance, so there wouldn't be any confusion. We weren't docked points for poor acting, so it was the least of my worries.

Inevitably, there was always a fire during the drill, so I would always make a mental note of where the extinguishers and smoke hoods were. There would also be at least one disruptive passenger on our fake plane, so I knew to be on the alert and suspect everyone. One year my instructor decided he'd have a foreign passenger act as the unruly one during my drill, and so he had her only speaking in Italian and pretending not to understand anything that was going on.

"You'll need to place your purse under the seat in front of you for take-off," I told her, not yet realizing she didn't understand English.

My group's scenario had commenced during a preparation for departure and then was to continue airborne. I was walking up the single aisle ensuring everyone's seatbelt was buckled, seat backs and tray tables were up, bags were secured, and bins were closed.

The lady with the purse looked up at me and yelled, "*Non toccare la mia borsa!*"

What the instructor failed to remember was that his unruly actor was not the only one who spoke Italian. She was mad that I had touched her purse, not understanding that I just wanted to secure it under the seat for take-off. His plan backfired when I was able to speak back to her in her tongue and calm her down rather quickly. I was never so glad to have been brought up speaking Italian. My fast-beating heart could now relax a little, as one problem had already been resolved.

All carry-on bags were always deemed suspicious, as at least one would prove to be problematic by either containing something it shouldn't, being left unattended, catching fire, or simply posing as a tripping hazard. Babies (dolls) tended to get stashed just about anywhere, so I would have to be sure to check under the seats before evacuating the aircraft, as moms would sometimes ditch their own children. I never heard of this happening in real life, but in our simulators, our acting moms and dads did it quite frequently. I'd like to say I would never do this myself; however, I did once climb over my mother after a car accident and left her behind.

Let me explain. Someone had crashed into my car on the driver side, which left me unable to open my door. Since a lot of smoke had built up in the car, I thought it was about to catch fire, so being six months pregnant at the time, my survival instinct kicked in, and my fat belly and I climbed over my mother who was seated in the passenger seat refusing to move. There were people coming from all directions, so I knew after being assisted from the car someone else would help my mother as well. As it turned out the smoke in the car was from the airbags having deployed, but at the time, I was obviously unaware of this. The ambulance took both of us to the hospital, and besides a big scare, burns from the airbags, major ugly bruising, and some soreness, we (including the baby) were fine, and my mother forgave me.

Back in the simulator I would pretend to look busy and stand by for an emergency, which was bound to happen sooner or later. The instructor enjoyed taunting us and would sometimes drag this out just to get our hearts pumping with anticipation. And then it would happen. It could be anything from a passenger with a medical condition to an explosion that ripped a hole in the fuselage. Regardless of the scenario, there was usually some form of smoke. Although, some years our scenarios were so basic that I'd be thrown off my game and just stand there with a confused look on my face. *That's it?* Most were more complicated, however, and entailed everything from demonstrations to personal briefings to securing everything and everyone, including those troublesome, unruly passengers. The cabin would get prepared for an evacuation, and then we'd buckle ourselves in our jump seats and anxiously await the brace-for-impact command. Next were the various recorded sounds of yelling, crying, wind gushing, or engines roaring and then silence and dimness—except for the lighting from the emergency exit signs and floor strips. Finally, like a musical conductor orchestrating his band, everything would fall into place, and we'd evacuate all the passengers from this now smoke-ridden aircraft simulator making sure no one had been left behind. If during an evacuation passengers hesitated to jump onto a slide when at the emergency door, we were then permitted to push them. Maybe I should have pushed my mother out of the car?

At any rate, after the simulator drills were completed, our instructors would review everything that was done correctly but more so, incorrectly. One year my airline even had video cameras placed in the simulator so they could replay our humiliation again and again. A couple of times I was made to act as the flight director. Even though these went surprisingly well, I would still never want to hold that responsibility. I had no ambition of being in charge. In fact, even when crew sked asked if I would upgrade to flight director for certain flights in need, I would pass it off to the next down in seniority.

Upon completion of the scenarios everyone tended to breathe a sigh of relief. The rest of the day was relatively easy in comparison. There was a fire-fighting drill in which we would assemble outdoors, don a smoke hood, grab a fire extinguisher, and discharge water at a small controlled, gas flame and then each strut away like we ruled the place because we successfully put out a fire.

My father could have used some fire safety training the year he invited my family and I over for a Father's Day lunch. My husband and I knew something was wrong when we were nearly at his house and saw smoke billowing in the air and could smell something burning. This wasn't the first time he had burnt chicken on the BBQ, so we weren't overly concerned. This time, however, he did more than just burn the chicken. He thought it was a good idea to use charcoal on his propane barbeque but then also place it near the entrance of a fabric canopy with mesh screening. It ended up catching fire and consequently melting the canopy. I think we then may have ordered a pizza instead.

Then there was the raft. We had to inflate our life jackets, remove our shoes, and huddle into an inflatable raft. We would take turns demonstrating all the gadgets associated with the raft and discuss the how-to and what-if scenarios. The fun was when we had to work together in erecting the raft's canopy. While we were all still uncomfortably sitting in the raft with our jackets inflated, making it difficult to turn our necks, the instructor would throw the folded-up canopy into the centre and tell us to set it up. The person closest to it would start to unravel it while the rest of us would begin grabbing an end. We'd usually have to pass it around a couple of times before finding the correct side, since the opening had to be where the boarding station was. It was kind of like a group of people sitting on a large air mattress playing parachute except it needed to be properly attached. The canopy had strings that needed to be tied around the outside perimeter of the raft, which meant awkwardly hanging over the sides, butts in the air while those closest to the middle part were securing it over a centre support mast. Trying to scooch around the raft on our butts with an inflated jacket and slippery socks wasn't exactly the smoothest operation. We tended to bump and slide into one another before a successful erection (of the canopy).

The use of equipment found on our aircraft would also be reviewed. This included the donning of the infant life jackets by using the abandoned babies from the simulator. The operation of emergency doors and windows was mandated as well as our individual evacuation drills. This meant reciting bilingual, shouted commands according to the aircraft and type of emergency assigned—whether it be a land or a ditch* evacuation. We'd start by sitting on our jump seats. I had to make sure the seat belt was well adjusted, so it needed to be tight and low. Depending on my direction on the aircraft, my head was either pushed back into the headrest or dropped forward with my chin down. My feet were placed together and slightly forward, and my hands were resting on top of my legs by my knees. Signaling the thumbs up to the instructor meant I was now in position to start. I was so nervous one year that I couldn't remember how to say shoes in French. At least I had thought I couldn't. When my instructor saw that I stopped midway through my commands and asked why, he told me I had already said *soulieres* and to keep going. Since I was on autopilot mode, I hadn't even realized it. Next, the door would be opened, the tag to inflate the slide or slide raft would be in my hand (more acting), and the pretend passengers would be evacuated. I'd do a final check of the cabin, and once satisfied no one was left on board, I, too, would jump out the door. If all the steps were done correctly, I was free to move on and send in the next "victim." If not, I'd be allowed a redo. I had to redo it once when I forgot to inflate my own life jacket before leaving the aircraft.

Naturally training day would not be complete without group discussions, which were designed to make us work as a team. Once, we had to compete in an escape room type game. It was basically a briefcase, a canister, a carry-on luggage, and a service trolley. The briefcase held various forms and pamphlets that we would normally find on the aircraft as well as specific flight plans that only the pilots understood. The canister housed cups, dishes, and utensils with letters taped underneath. The luggage contained items you would use at a beach, such as sunshades and a toy shovel, and the trolley was locked with a combination lock. Normally I was competitive, but I was ready to wave a white flag almost immediately after we started. I rifled through the briefcase with another flight attendant while others tried their luck looking for clues in the luggage and canister. The pilot in our group eventually stepped up and was able to decipher the flight plan from the briefcase to lead us to our next clue, but that was pretty much as far as we got without additional aid. Our instructor took pity on my group and gave us way too many hints. Even with all the extra hints, my group still managed to fail. I think it was rigged. At any rate, the day would eventually come to an end, and I would be qualified to fly for at least another year—unless I still needed to recertify my first aid and CPR that same year then that would be another "fun-filled" day.

First aid and CPR training was just standard instruction in a classroom full of dummies. It included everything from a minor wound to the use of the AED – automated external defibrillator. My favourite part of the day was making doughnuts (also called ring pads). With the use of a triangular bandage, we would fold and loop it into a circle so that it looked like a doughnut. This was used to immobilize impaled objects. Even though I was trained it was still always frightening when someone truly needed help, especially if that someone was family.

After my daughter's choking incident in a restaurant, I had gotten myself so worked up that the paramedic who had arrived told me that both me and my daughter should get ourselves checked out at the hospital. She needed to be checked for possible fluid in her lungs, and I needed to be checked because I was pregnant, and my blood pressure had skyrocketed. We ended up being fine, but I never allowed my daughter to eat mints again.

As much as I absolutely dreaded this training day every year, I'd put on my big girl pants and get it done. If I wanted to keep flying, it was part of the job. The good thing about my annual was that I was always in the first batch of training dates for the year, so after mine was completed I could just chill and watch as others would be nervously reviewing in preparation while at work. Training had prepared me for possible cases of emergencies, but what it hadn't trained me for were the everyday in-flight situations. Like the time someone vomitted all over my jump seat before landing and then just left me to deal with it or even simple service training, like preparing the specialty coffees in club class.

The Lingo

Communication took on a whole new dimension as a flight attendant. Crew lingo included flight attendant slang or sign language, the phonetic alphabet, airline codes, the 24-hour clock, Zulu time, and certain signs and terminology. Acronyms and abbreviations were also used daily.

When out in the middle of the aisles with the trolleys or assisting passengers, it was sometimes difficult to relay what you needed from your fellow colleagues from a distance. Thus, the flight attendant sign language was born.

The following is a crash course on some of the more popular hand gestures. If you found yourself in the aisle and needed something for your passenger, you had to first catch the attention of a fellow flight attendant in the back galley. This could be achieved by either pressing the passenger call light repeatedly until you annoyed the flight attendant enough to look in your direction or, if they'd already looked towards you, you could simply wave your arms and proceed with the appropriate sign. Not all the flight attendants would be at the same level of communication, as there was no set handbook or formal training. It was something learned through experience, so if your galley attendant was a newbie, they might return your gesture with a confused look, wondering what's wrong with you. Similarly, the passengers would sometimes give you odd looks, particularly if requesting more Coke (you'll see why shortly). Other times, passengers would find it clever and amusing. You just had to be aware if you had any hearing-impaired passengers on board because this could result in an embarrassing situation.

One such embarrassing experience happened when I was in the aisles assisting with boarding and one of the passengers asked me for an extension seat belt. Because I was boxed in and couldn't head to the back to grab one myself, I caught the attention of a colleague and made the appropriate hand gesture so she would know what I needed her to relay. Immediately after my request, a passenger waiting to take his seat performed a different hand gesture. I thought he just wanted to play along, so I returned a random hand motion, which meant nothing at all. Then his expression grew sullen. He wasn't playing. He was indeed hearing impaired and was making a real request. I didn't know if what I had motioned was offensive or if he was just upset that I couldn't truly sign. Either way, I was mortified and didn't use any hand gestures for the rest of the flight.

Back to the crash course. For milk you would simply pretend you were milking a cow. For 7UP you formed the number seven with your thumb and index finger and then flipped your wrist. Coke was communicated with a finger under the nose while tilting your head backwards, as in the motion for snorting cocaine. (Don't do drugs!) For diet drinks you drew the outline of an hourglass (indicating a curvaceous body) before adding it to the 7UP or Coke signal. Coffee was requested by forming the letter *C* with one hand, and tea was requested by touching the palm of one hand to the fingers of the other hand, thus both forming the letter *T*. For apple juice you would pretend to pick an apple off a tree and take a bite into it. Orange juice was simply formed by making the letter *O* with one hand. Water and ice did not require the use of hand gestures, as you could simply request them by holding up the jug or tongs, respectively. Unless of course you did not have a beverage trolley in front of you, in which case you would ask for water by forming the letter *W* with the three middle fingers of one hand. Whereas for ice, you pretended you were freezing by wrapping your arms around yourself and shaking side to side. For Iced Tea you would combine the ice sign with the tea sign. Sometimes flight attendants would attempt to hold up an empty can instead of performing the sign language, but unless you were close by, it was too difficult to differentiate between the soft drinks.

Aside from the drink signs, we also had signs for meal choices. Chicken was signaled by placing your hands under your armpits and flapping your arms up and down. For beef you placed your index fingers at each side of your temple, as if they were horns. For pasta you used one hand to form the straight line of the *P* while the other hand formed a half circle at the top of the first hand, thus forming the letter *P*. When in need of utensils, you would use both hands and pretend you were shoveling food into your mouth.

Flight attendants extended their sign language to items beyond food, such as seatbelt extensions and pens. For the seat belt you would hold both arms up in the air and, with closed fists, knock them together two times. (According to my daughter this sign was also known as Ross flipping off Monica in the show *Friends*.) When you needed a pen, you would pretend to be writing something in the air by placing your thumb and index fingers together and folding the rest of the fingers into your palm. The next time you're on a plane, you'll be in the know, and you may even be able to save a flight attendant from taking unnecessary steps when you can simply sign your request from afar.

The phonetic alphabet was heard most frequently in the cockpit, particularly in relation to airline codes. It also came in handy when spelling out names and not wanting to mess them up or just wanting to prove that you, too, could *tango-alpha-lima-kilo* like a pilot. Another clever use was for cursing politely with none the wiser, as in *foxtrot oscar* (fuck off); although most flight attendants still preferred to swear in the classic fashion once in the privacy of the galley. The only passengers I ever heard use this alphabet were the older ones who were once travel agents or pilots. It was as if they were happy to be somewhere where they could use it and be understood, even if it was just to read their seat number out loud. A little bit of practice and you'd be *alpha* to *zuluing* in no time. (The following is the alphabet so you can get started with your learning: *alpha, bravo, charlie, delta, echo, foxtrot, golf, hotel, india, juliet, kilo, lima, mike, november, oscar, papa, quebec, romeo, sierra, tango, uniform, victor, whiskey, x-ray, yankee, zulu*.)

Airport codes were three-letter codes used to identify the different airports throughout the world, and, similarly, two-letter codes were used to identify the different airlines. Pre-ordered meals were distinguished with a four-letter code. Every aircraft also had its own unique code. The airport codes became the city names for crew, so if someone were to ask where we were headed, for example, we would never say Punta Cana but instead would say Pooge, as in the code PUJ. Many airport codes could not be sounded out as easily, however, so the letters would just be said instead, such as Y-V-R for Vancouver. Some codes became fun words, like the one for FLL (Fort Lauderdale) that turned into the word *Fa-la-la*. Like much of the crew lingo, this was not something taught, but rather experienced. The more routes you'd work, the more you'd pick up.

The special meals (and the codes associated with them) that passengers would sometimes pre-order were quite simple to decipher. VGML, for example, meant vegan meal, not to be confused with VLML, however, which meant vegetarian lacto ovo meal and therefore included eggs and dairy. It would not be out of the ordinary to hear, "Throw the diabetic in the oven for a few more minutes," because the DBML (diabetic meal) was not warm enough. No one thought twice when a colleague would announce, "I'm missing a Muslim," because we were short on the pre-ordered MOML (Muslim meal). When we were preparing the special meals, we were still in the galley and not yet out in the aisles, which meant we tended to be out of passenger earshot, so luckily I never came across anyone getting offended by these sometimes-questionable phrases. Eventually most meals became one and the same, so it wouldn't matter if you ordered the vegetarian, the diabetic, or the low-fat option—you were getting the same crap (I meant meal).

Because I worked on many different aircraft and it would sometimes become confusing to differentiate them by just a code, many would get nicknamed by relating their code name with a specific characteristic about it. So, for example we would say something like TV-crap instead of TVC to remind us it was that shitty aircraft no one liked working on.

I've listed and explained the airline acronyms and abbreviations I used most often, unless already used elsewhere in this book, in which case it has been explained as it appears.

OPS: Short for flight operations, this does not refer to performing surgery in flight but rather a group of people that help everything run smoothly and efficiently at an airport.

PAX: This is short for passenger.

PIC: This refers to the pilot in command, otherwise known as captain or left seater.

F/O: This refers to the first officer, otherwise known as second-in-command or right seater (they really don't appreciate being called second-in-command).

F/D: This refers to the flight director, otherwise known as the in-charge or purser (not to be confused with the flight instrument used in a cockpit).

F/A: This refers to a flight attendant, not to be confused with the phrase "fuck all," such as when someone asks you what you're up to and you answer, "sweet fuck all."

UM: Not as in when you don't know what to say, but rather this refers to an unaccompanied minor.

YP: Not as in your problem, but rather this refers to a young person, a passenger travelling alone who is too old to be a UM but too young to be considered an adult.

TOD: This is short for the time of departure.

Airlines liked to emphasize that effective communication was key when working with your crew, so being familiar with the lingo, codes, terminology, and so on will only strengthen your abilities. The use of signing would facilitate services by not having to guess what was needed and even added a little entertainment for the passengers. Being knowledgeable in the different forms of flight attendant communication also created a bond of camaraderie. It was like being part of a secret club, and who didn't like that? As a side note, if your goal was to one day become a pilot, you might want to increase your usage of crutch words, such as *uh*, *um*, and *er*, as they seemed to use these quite frequently over the P.A. system.

You may want to return to the test below after you have completed reading this book to learn more definitions first.

> **Test question:**
> If crew sked were to call at thirteen hundred with a new TOD of twenty-two ten Zulu for a deadhead on alpha Zulu 1475 from FCO to Mobay, but then OPS sent a cancellation update because the PIC accidentally popped a slide, so instead you now had to ferry to Pop, which meant no PAX and you could sit at fifteen echo and eat the unclaimed diabetic. But unfortunately when you arrived, the aircraft was grounded, thereby getting released, but then you slipped and ended up requiring a straight back and were told to standby, what would you do?

The Commute

Over the course of my flying career, I've seen many changes, including that of my physical appearance as I became a more experienced flight attendant, and the journey it would take to arrive at my gate. The pristine flight attendant look I was so keen on maintaining when I was first hired, started taking a back seat to sleep. Strategic conveniences began playing a lead role. In contrast, my commute to work was becoming ever more inconvenient the bigger and busier the airport became.

When I first wore my uniform, I was young and unmarried (my now hubby was my then boyfriend). I still had the time and energy to dedicate to my appearance. As much as my hair went through many stages, from truly short to awfully long and everything in between, I always gave it enough attention to not look dishevelled. I was never big on makeup, but I would still try to add a little colour and contour. I would spray on a little bit of perfume and make sure my heels were polished, my uniform wasn't wrinkled, and my neck scarf was neatly tied.

Years later, I was married with three children and a dog. Life had now become about strategy and sleep. My hair was purposely kept just short enough (above the collar) to not have to pull back into a ponytail or bun but still long enough to not have to style. I could simply roll out of bed. Since I have naturally wavy hair, I figured I could play up the tousled look. My makeup was traded in for a simple lip chap. Deodorant was my current perfume of choice. My heels went into storage the moment they were no longer deemed mandatory. I now had my sensible flats, which, with a quick swipe of a wet hand wipe, were good to go. I chose to wear the sweater option versus the blouse (even in the summer months), so that I wouldn't have to iron, and the neck scarf was knotted without a second thought. This way, when my alarm would sound at the all-too-familiar time of 0300 hours, for instance, I could be dressed and ready to go in as little as fifteen minutes. Strategy.

Staff parking at the airport had also undergone some drastic changes over the years. At the beginning I would park in a nearby airport lot, stand by my car or keep my lights on if dark, and wait for a shuttle bus to drive me to the terminal. Shelters were eventually constructed, which meant having to wait with other employees at various locations scattered throughout the lot instead. As the airport continued to grow, construction ensued, and space became limited, we were consequently juggled around until we eventually moved to a parking garage connected to the terminals by ways of link trains.

As much as going to work while the rest of the world slept was depressing, it did have its advantages. No traffic. Okay, that's about it. The no-traffic perk, however, existed only until I arrived at the airport staff parking, and then it was complete pandemonium. Like vultures circling for prey, cars were screeching around corners searching for that one empty spot. When I had bought myself a small car, I was so excited to drive it to work because I could easily park this cute, little thing just about anywhere with ease. The lesson I quickly learned, however, was that yes, I could park it in tight spaces, but no, I could not physically exit the vehicle once in that tight spot.

This stalking-type activity in the parking garage was pretty much an all day, everyday occurrence, particularly during the winter season as everyone attempted to avoid parking outdoors. If I ran out of time to keep circling for an indoor spot and had no choice but to park outside, all I could do was hope my car wasn't buried under a mountain of snow or completely frozen by the time I returned.

I was so tired after one of my flights that I accepted a ride to my car from one of these "stalkers" one day. Everyone who works at the airport must have a background check, so I knew she at least had some credibility. When she saw me exit the doors leading to the garage, she asked if she could follow me to my car to guarantee her my parking spot. When I told her that it was at the far corner of the garage, she offered me a lift. After a quick scan, I figured I could take her if push came to shove, and I hopped in. It was a win-win. I was secured a quick, warm ride, and she was secured a parking spot. Please do not shake your head at me. I was tired.

Securing a parking spot did not mean my destination was close by. This just meant I was one step closer to completing my trek to the gate. The next step was the walk through the garage, which, depending on how lucky I was, could be anywhere from a few seconds to a few minutes, and if that walk was from the outdoor lot, add some extra minutes. After then crossing a skywalk I would arrive at the link trains, which shuttled me to the terminal. There were two trains that ran alternately on one line, so it didn't matter which you took because both went to the two terminals. Without fail, one of these trains was always under maintenance, which would add even more time on the commute.

Strikes were not an uncommon occurrence at the airport; however, when the strikers chose to picket at the staff parking gates, the already hectic garage became a nightmare. Lineups were forming well before the gates could even be seen, as the strikers, in their protesting attempts, would hold up every vehicle trying to enter. During this time, I had to add an extra hour onto my commute. Lateness was still inexcusable with my job.

In all my years of flying, I had never been late—although sometimes extremely close. I had been brought up to always be early or, at the very least, on time. It was ingrained in me as a kid, and I've never been able to shake it. I started to sweat if I felt I was going to be late for something. It's like I was being raised to become a flight attendant. I was not sure how it was with other airlines; however, with my company, it was basically a three-strikes-you're-out kind of thing or, at the very least, time to involve your union rep. When lateness with flight crew did happen, the rest of us would have to step up and do what we could to prepare the plane until that person showed or until a replacement had arrived. Sometimes this meant having to delay the flight, (which angered *everyone*). As long as it wasn't a pilot we were waiting for, we would fly with one fewer person (which angered the cabin crew).

My commute didn't end once I was finally at my respective terminal—it was now time to go through security. The employee entrance was where a security officer would sit and watch as everyone wearing a badge would either scan their fingerprint or their eye to proceed. I would inevitably have to rely on the retinal scanner because apparently my fingerprints were too faint and could not be read. If I did have to go through security somewhere in which I had no option but to use my fingerprints, it would turn into phone calls, leafing through binders, or extra searches. In some cases, I would be sent back through the regular passenger security line. If I was able to proceed, next came the press-your-luck button.

Everyone passing through security had to press this lovely red button. If your light turned green, you were good to pass on through. Red meant all your bags, coats, shoes, phones, keys, belts, change, watches, and so on must be placed on the conveyor belt and pass through the X-ray machine for inspection. Of course, this always seemed to happen most frequently during the winter months when I wore extra articles of clothing, such as a hat, a scarf, and boots. When going through the metal detector I would just hope not to set it off. I'd pat myself down making sure I didn't forget anything and wait for security to waive me through as I'd watch my items move along the conveyor.

"Next!" commanded the security officer one winter morning.

Please don't beep, please don't beep, I thought while holding my breath. As if breathing too heavily would cause the alarms to go off. *Beep, beep, beep!* I had somehow managed to anger the metal detector gods.

"I'll need you to spread out your arms and legs, ma'am."

And I'll need to throat punch you, I wanted to reply to the officer, but of course I just stood there frozen. I could feel my face turn more and more red as the officer waved her wand across my body. When she passed it over my chest, it caused the wand to get a little excited. This was the day I learned that the underwire in certain bras could trigger sensitive metal detectors. It would also be the start of my wire-free bra collection. My experience with this stranger and her happy wand was not exactly enjoyable for someone who hated being in the spotlight.

Sometimes it was the bag going through the X-ray machine that was the issue. Leaving from my home base as an air crew member, I was permitted to bring my own water through security; however, sometimes security wouldn't realize I was a flight attendant until they had already pulled my bag aside to inspect. This was always an easy fix. The problem was when I was returning from Scotland. Since crew were expected to follow the same tight carry-on restrictions as passengers, I always made sure to follow the rules. So when my bag was pulled aside at security, I was confused as to why. When the security officer asked me to open my carry-on luggage in front of him, all I could think of were my dirty underwear and smelly shoes. I watched in horror as he rifled through my personal belongings, feeling my face turn red. Normally I placed my dirties in a separate, small ditty bag, but because *all* my clothes had to be washed, and I wasn't expecting someone to go through them, I hadn't bothered. The smelly shoes I had in there were my old galley shoes that were well over due to be replaced but hadn't gotten around to and so seemed to retain their odour from all my previous flights. After this humiliating search, security discovered that it was, in fact, my colleague's bag, which was directly behind mine on the conveyor belt, that was setting off the alarm and not mine. As it turned out, he forgot to remove his laptop.

After being vigorously scrutinized in the security area, it was now time to search for my gate. Was it going to be a close-by gate conveniently located next to a coffee shop, or was it going to be one that required some speed walking or possibly even a bus to get to? If it was close, easy. I'd have enough time to browse through the duty-free boutiques, spray on some free perfume, moisturize my hands with some complimentary cream samples, and grab a coffee all before going to the aircraft. If, however, it was at a gate all the way at the opposite end of the airport, I would have to sprint down two sets of escalators, then across two moving sidewalks (which by the way if someone was going to simply stand on, they had better do so to the side or face the wrath of my luggage trying to push past), then up an escalator, up another escalator, and finally, once out of breath, sweating, and rosy-cheeked, I would arrive. If I sprinted fast enough, I could still grab a coffee. It didn't matter if my hair was dishevelled, my uniform needed to be readjusted, or people were staring at me as I ran past them, as long as I made it to the gate on time and preferably with a coffee in hand.

The worst gate option was the one in which a bus was required. This meant going down an escalator into a holding area to wait for a bus, which would then load as many people waiting as it could hold. Not surprisingly it was always packed with only standing room available by the time I was able to squeeze my way in. The bus ride was approximately seven minutes of my trying desperately not to land on a stranger as it would quickly swirl around and eventually make its way to our secluded infield concourse. Once there, I had yet another escalator to climb. The most I could ask for here was something from the vending machine, as they hadn't bothered to put any coffee shops (or anything else for that matter) in this area of the airport. Regardless of which gate I had to get to, I knew I'd soon enough be meeting up with my herd in my home away from home—my special tin can in the sky. The adventure was about to begin.

Although the whole process of going through security and arriving at my gate at my home base was sometimes agonizingly painful, it was still not the worst I had experienced. I used to travel to a cruise destination airport in which it seemed everyone was sweaty, and no one wore socks. Going through security meant everyone, including crew, had to remove their shoes, and because it was always so packed, the foot odour was enough to make a baby elephant pass out. Luckily, our uniforms were well equipped. Our neck scarves were a perfect accessory that not only looked professional but also doubled as a face mask. They proved invaluable once again when one of the airports I often frequented was dealing with a mouse infestation in their ceilings. This misfortune took months to resolve, but, luckily for me, I had my trusty double-duty scarf. (Ironically enough, this airport was home to one of the world's most famous mice.) As inconvenient as my commuting might have been at times, it was still nothing in comparison to some of my colleagues who commuted from out of the country. Kudos to those guys for their dedication. My twenty-minute drive, which could sometimes turn into two hours, was the extent I was willing to travel before flying off somewhere.

*ditch: Not as in a narrow hole in the ground, or what I did to my mother when I left her alone in my car after the accident, but rather this is when an aircraft makes an emergency landing on water.

*Zulu time: Also known as Universal Coordinated Time (UCT) or Greenwich Mean Time (GMT), this is the time at zero meridian, which is based in Greenwich, England (for example: if it's 0634EST, it's 1134Z).

Chapter Five

The Planes (and Yes, the Lavatories)

Those tin cans you saw flying in the sky were my travelling office. They safely carried me and my passengers on countless journeys. But if you were to ask me the mechanics or specifications of that aircraft, I'd have to refer you to someone else. Here's what I *did* know about planes: they were mostly made of aluminum, used a "magical" force called lift to fly (thanks to the air flowing over the wings when the plane was moving forward at high speed), and were the fastest and safest mode of travel.

Some passengers, as well as certain colleagues, were truly knowledgeable on the specifics of certain aircraft, and then there were those who needed assistance opening the door to the lavatory (which I will get to shortly). My knowledge was limited more to the inside of the cabin. For instance, I could provide you with a half decent coffee, work the entertainment unit, set the mood lighting, find your seat, and most importantly save your butt in case of an emergency. My skills in relation to planes rested primarily on service and rescue. So when the pilots would tell us that the passengers had to remain seated in their assigned seats prior to take off for weight and balance purposes, I never questioned them. And when they would ask us to move some of the larger passengers on smaller aircraft, this got tricky but was usually well handled (by the juniors).

I worked on numerous types of planes over the years, including Lockheed L-1011s; Boeing 727s, 737s, and 757s; and Airbus A310s, A320s, A321s, and A330s. I preferred working on some more than others, but I found they all had their pros and cons. The Lockheeds, for example, offered a getaway in the lower galley, but on the downside, I had to deal with the mushrooms. The smaller, narrow-bodied aircraft held fewer passengers, so boarding and deplaning tended to be quicker, but having only one aisle sometimes meant having to dance around people and trolleys to pass. The wide-bodied aircraft with two aisles made it easier to get around, but everything seemed to take longer, and more crew and passengers usually also meant more issues.

The aircraft used for destinations were chosen according to their fuel range and carrying capacity, so when I would request specific routes, I would usually end up working on similar types of aircraft. Some flight attendants would factor in which aircraft they'd be working on when building their schedule. I was usually more interested in the day and destination; although this would prove challenging to switch with others at times, if the majority did not enjoy working on my scheduled aircraft.

Passenger seating was such a common issue that the seats themselves needed to be discussed, and since I practically lived inside a plane's cabin, I can offer my expertise in this area. The seat numbers were assigned according to their row in the aircraft, so if yours was number five, for example, you're obviously in the fifth row. Unless there was a club class, like on some of the aircraft I worked, in which case you would be in the third row, which was also the first row of economy. Regardless, you got the idea—the higher the number, the farther back you went. (Fun fact: certain airlines have chosen to remove row thirteen due to the superstition that the number is considered unlucky.)

The letters associated with the row number represented your position in that row, starting with *A* on the left-hand side of the plane and moving right. *A* and *K* were always window seats, but on certain aircraft, *F* was also a window seat. *C*, *D*, and *H* were always aisle seats, but *F* and *G* could be aisle seats as well. The letters were dependent on the configuration of the aircraft. The letter *I* did not exist because it could be confused with the number 1. Sometimes there would be an aircraft switch, and passengers would come on board with a row that didn't exist on the new aircraft. Their assigned seat on the previous aircraft would be where the lavatory was on the current aircraft, for instance. Many passengers were good sports when this happened and just laughed it off, as the ground agent would then assign them a new seat.

When assisting with boarding from the last set of doors, I used to ask passengers what their seat *letter* was so I could guide them to the right side of the aircraft. The row number did not matter because we were at the far back, and unless their seat was in the galley or in the lavatory, there was no choice but to walk forward up the aisle. Inevitably most would answer with a number.

"Welcome, can I see your boarding card please?" I had asked yet another one of the passengers stepping on board, who was obviously part of the same wedding party as the ones I had already seen because she was wearing a matching neon green shirt that read "Mom of the Bride."

Most passengers would hold their boarding card in their hands until they were at their assigned seat, but there were always those who buried it so deep in their bag, they'd have to rifle through all their belongings before finding it at the bottom. This mom was the latter.

She rummaged through her bag while mumbling under her breath, "I know it's here somewhere." I stood there waiting. *How do you misplace something that the gate agent literally just checked one minute ago before you walked on the bridge?* Others behind her still waiting to board must have been thinking the same thing because the look on their faces became that of annoyance.

I was just about to ask her to step aside while she continued looking so that we could proceed with the boarding when suddenly she exclaimed, "Got it!"

"Great," I said.

I took a quick glance at her card to ensure she belonged on our aircraft (as per the rules, even though her shirt had already unofficially told me she did) and before I could tell her where she was seated (31K), she quickly snatched the card back and said, "I know where I'm going." As she was walking away, I asked her to confirm her seat letter. "31," she replied and proceeded up the wrong aisle.

For tall passengers or those simply wishing for more leg space, the bulkhead seats or even the emergency exit rows provided the most room to stretch out your legs. The bulkheads either had a wall or a curtain in front, which was used to divide those seats from either another cabin class, a galley, or a lavatory. Many bulkhead seats also offered the use of a baby bassinet. The downfall to a bulkhead seat was that it didn't typically offer storage under a seat in front and was a popular area for parents with their babies. Unless you liked babies, then it's where you didn't want to be. Passengers sitting in an emergency exit row seat also had to be physically capable and willing to assist in the event of an emergency. Fair warning: these seats tended to be the coldest area of the plane and didn't always recline.

For those who experienced motion sickness, had connecting flights, or simply wanted to leave faster upon arrival, sitting at the front of the aircraft would be your best option—particularly the aisle seat—for the quickest exit. Sitting near a lavatory was only recommended if you required frequent visits, as it had more noise and smells, and tended to get busy with passengers lining up. For those looking to sleep or take in the views, the window seats would be ideal. You could use the wall to lean up against and nap, and you also had control of the window shade. The downfall was when you had to excuse yourself to get past your neighbours. (By the way, not all window seats had a window.) Besides being the last to exit (except when stairs and multiple doors were used at certain destinations), those seated in the back of the aircraft would feel the most movements of the plane and would probably hear the most noise, as both the galley and the lavatories were usually in the rear. The flight crew working and chatting in the galley might also get a little loud at times. But if you were the party type, the back was where it was at.

Even if you weren't the party type, you've likely found yourself at the back of a plane at one point or another, bringing me to this next (very important) topic: the lavatories. You wouldn't think that I would have to dedicate a whole section on lavatories, specifically how to open an aircraft's lavatory door, and yet, here it was. On the aircraft I've worked on, we had two types of doors: the traditional swinging door and the accordion style. Both were uncomplicated, but somehow, they still caused many passengers to struggle.

The traditional type is a single door with a handle that opens outward. Seemed simple enough. I think many passengers unnecessarily thought it to be more complicated than it was intended. It was like watching someone who was trying to think outside the box when the answer was clearly right in front of them. Because our aircraft still legally had to come furnished with ashtrays, even though smoking was banned on board, these small metal ashtrays were placed on the outside of many of the lavatory walls. (The reason they still existed on aircraft was so that there was a safe place to dispose of the cigarette if a yahoo were to light up.) Pulling them down opened them up for usage. Sure enough, instead of using the door handle to open the lavatory, passengers would continually open the ashtray to no avail. I'd constantly be closing the ashtrays every time I'd pass the lavatories. Besides the ever-popular ashtray handle, I once witnessed a passenger frantically waving his hands around the front of the door. I soon discovered that he thought it was like those automatic doors at the entrance of a mall.

The accordion-type doors were also a lot simpler to open than many passengers realized. All that was required was a push inward towards the centre of the door and voilà it folded itself open. It was so easy to open, in fact, that when passengers *weren't* purposely attempting to open it, it would. If you leaned up against the door, you could find yourself unintentionally in the lavatory. This occurred on many occasions when passengers were standing in the aisles waiting to disembark and someone would inevitably get tired of waiting and lean up against the door, not knowing they'd end up in the lavatory. I had to admit that I, too, after a long day, found myself in the lavatory. It was therefore ironic when passengers intentionally wanting to use the lavatory weren't able to figure out how to open this type of door. I'd see them trying to pry it open from the side, looking feverishly for a handle, or turning to the nearest person in search of assistance.

Regardless of which aircraft passengers were on, the common difficulty sometimes came with simply finding the lavatory. Cupboards were often mistaken for lavatories. This wouldn't have been too weird if the cupboards weren't roughly one foot wide by two feet high. Some of the closets were large enough to house jackets, but even those we'd have to wonder what the passenger was thinking. Airplane lavatories were small, but you needed to at least be able to stand in the space.

Knowing how to open the door was one thing but knowing when it was occupied was another. Just because a passenger was familiar with the complicated mechanics of opening the door, it did not secure them the use of said lavatory. When the door was locked by someone on the inside, the sign by the lavatory ceiling would illuminate red to indicate that it was occupied. If the light was green, it was vacant and therefore available. Aside from this, there was an actual mechanism on the front of the door—usually by the handle—that would slide into place and indicate red for busy or green for free. Some even spelled out the words *occupied* or *vacant*. So no matter how much someone pulled on that door, if it was occupied, it was locked. Unless of course it was occupied and the passenger neglected to lock it, which did happen quite frequently. I would unknowingly open the lavatory door only to find a passenger with their pants down. This was usually followed by shrieking from both parties, my slamming the door shut, and yelling, "lock the door!" Therefore, lock the door. This would not only ensure your privacy but also illuminate the lights.

As flight attendants we can open locked lavatories from the outside by ways of a secret technique. This came in handy on numerous occasions when little children locked themselves in and didn't know how to get out. Typically, it was children who needed help; however, I did have to unlock the door for a few elderly passengers, who would then exit feeling embarrassed. Once I unlocked the door for an elderly gentleman who was obviously not ready to exit because his pants were still around his ankles. It sounded like he needed help because he was banging on the door, so when I asked him through the door if he was stuck and he didn't answer, I thought maybe he had hurt himself. It turned out he was hard of hearing, and the banging was just him trying to change his pants in extremely tight quarters.

If you really needed to use the lavatory on the plane, it was best to do so at the beginning of the flight and not towards the end because as much as the flight attendants were supposed to tidy them up every so often, they did get increasingly nasty as more and more passengers used them. Hundreds of passengers were using the same lavatory, which only got a quick two-minute cleaning by groomers when on the ground. You might want to think twice the next time you wanted to use a plane's lavatory without shoes or—gag—without socks. I would personally use the club class lavatories because only a small number of passengers had access to these, but an economy passenger would have to share with possibly hundreds. If you had a small bladder and needed frequent visits to the lavatory, you might want to consider paying extra for an upgraded class.

Many people were not fans of the loud-sucking vacuum flush, especially children, and therefore chose not to flush. This was not only disgusting but also extremely inconsiderate to the following lavatory user. Even when my children were little, they would do their business and then run out of the door just as they flushed so it wouldn't suck them in. Please note, the toilet would not suck small children in. It would, however, suck in small items never to be seen again.

On one of my flights when I first started with the company I was working in the lower galley, and as such I required the use of my flight director's company keys to unlock the canisters and trolleys. I kept her keys in my apron pocket for convenience and safe keeping. It was a long flight and I had to use the lavatory, so I proceeded upstairs. I was readjusting my apron while the toilet was flushing, and before I knew it, the keys flew out of my pocket and down the toilet. Just like that, they were gone. Not only were the company's lock keys on there, but also my flight director's home and car keys. I stood there mortified, contemplating where I should send in my job application next. (By the way, the waste is not dumped into the air as certain television shows would have you believe but rather into a holding tank that gets serviced once on the ground.) The flight director was obviously not impressed and chose to give me the silent treatment for the rest of the flight, but thankfully I was not fired.

It would seem obvious to place used hand towels and any other garbage into the receptacle marked *trash*, but you'd be surprised at the pretty creative crevices that passengers would cram their garbage into in the lavatories. The receptacle was usually near the sink, either on the counter or on the side of the wall, and would have a flap that you simply had to push. As much as I appreciated parents using the lavatory to change their baby's diaper, the dirty diaper left on top of the counter instead of inside the garbage bin was much less appreciated. Using the call button in the lavatory when assistance was not, in fact, needed was also not appreciated. And while on the topic of things that were unappreciated, I couldn't forget to mention the passengers who would leave feces or vomit spattered in the lavatories, which would then render that lavatory out of service for the duration of the flight. Think of that when you think of the glamorous job of a flight attendant.

This section would not be complete without talking about the mile-high-club passengers. First, one mile was 5,280 feet, so when flying over 36,000 feet you had already badly overshot this. Secondly, as discussed earlier, the lavatories were gross. If you were dead set on ignoring points one and two, then having one come out of the lavatory pretending like nothing happened while the other remained inside only to exit a few minutes later was not exactly fooling anyone. I was in the back galley with my colleagues enjoying my fifteenth coffee of the night (okay, slight exaggeration, it might have been my eleventh) on an overseas flight to Barcelona. We had recently finished our evening services and had the lights dimmed so the passengers could get a little shut-eye and we could get a break. While the crew and I were engaged in some company gossip, we saw a young woman with dishevelled hair sneaking out of the lavatory. The door "magically" closed on its own and locked itself back up again. Insert eye roll from the galley. Less than two minutes later, the door reopened, and a young man stepped out with the widest grin on his face. Insert laughter with a mix of gagging from the galley.

When in doubt about how to do something on a plane, such as open a lavatory door or even find a lavatory, all you had to do was ask. It was better than having the flight attendants watch and laugh later. On second thought, no, it wasn't. What would the crew have to talk about if you did?

To some, stepping into a giant tin can and trusting that it would safely fly you to your destination was nothing special, maybe even mundane. While to others, this form of travel might seem completely insane. Whether you fell into one of these categories or whether somewhere in between, if you were going to fly commercial, you might as well know how to find your seat, where you would be most comfortable sitting, and how to use the lavatories. And for the nervous travellers, let me assure you that even though flight attendants sometimes enjoyed teasing pilots who didn't know how to operate the simple gadgets in the galley in comparison to their ridiculous number of instruments in the cockpit, they were extremely skilled in their flying abilities—even when the first officer was the one landing the aircraft—despite their coffee-making skills.

Chapter Six

The Flights

There were two types of flying in a commercial airline: domestic and international. Within those types, however, there were a slew of further distinctions, particularly for flight attendants. These included turns, deadheads, ferries, direct, non-stop, connecting, standby, confirmed, jump seat, red-eyes, repatriation, military, humanitarian, and charity. Some of these were strictly geared towards flight crew, while others included passengers as well.

When flying domestically, the departure and arrival took place within the same country. This meant no duty-free shopping, no money exchanging, and no customs required upon landing. Even though these flights were relatively short, it did not mean that they were always turnarounds (a.k.a. turns). Sometimes I would bop around to different cities and return home days later, or I would start domestically but then had to travel internationally from a different city the next day. So, for example, I would fly Toronto to Vancouver one day, and the next I would have to fly from Vancouver to London, England. One of my favourite domestic turns used to be when we flew to Gander, Newfoundland and Labrador.

While the aircraft was being groomed for the return passengers, the crew would receive complimentary ice cream in our designated crew lounge there. Canadian East Coasters were the best.

Since international flying involved departing and arriving in different countries, this meant duty-free shopping was an option, money exchanging might be necessary, and customs was now mandatory. Depending on the duration of travel and whether extra fees were being charged for checked baggage, the overhead bins were either cramped or spacious. When I was travelling to New York City with my family for four days, there was no way we were paying extra for checked baggage, since the short flight was already ridiculously priced. So instead we each brought our own carry-on luggage, and, since the airline offered pre-boarding for families with small children, we boarded first and occupied two bins for ourselves. Travelling was expensive, so I didn't blame passengers when they tried to avoid paying for checked baggage fees on top of everything else as long as they were still within their carry-on limits.

Operating an international turn usually meant I was flying to the Caribbean. This would entail keeping paper towels on hand at my jump seat as sometimes passengers would end up taking unexpected showers caused by the condensation. The warm, humid air from outside would meet our cool aircraft, causing it to occasionally leak water through into the cabin and onto our unsuspecting passengers. It was harmless and most didn't even mind as I'd pass the paper towels along to those in need. Another common sight when flying from a hot and humid destination was the smoke or fog in the cabin. Sometimes it felt like you were walking into a nightclub and passengers either found it fun or frightening. When the aircraft's air conditioning was being blasted and the doors were opened, the cool air would mix with the outside air and result in a smoky-mist condition in the cabin. The more humid it was, the more mist we'd see, but it was usually quite short-lived as the aircraft cooled down once again. The more nervous travellers would think it was smoke from a fire but once reassured, they, too, found it to be fun. Caribbean turns meant one more thing for flight attendants: a thirty-minute tan. (Not for me, though, because as you will soon discover, the sun and I don't get along.)

. . .

When I first started flying, I used to operate many turns to Las Vegas (LAS). These flights were so hectic because on top of all our regular services, we always offered amazing deals on duty-free alcohol that everyone felt compelled to buy, so we'd be scrambling to get all the orders completed before landing. I didn't mind the rush because this meant there was no time to be bored, and besides, the Las Vegas airport offered frozen yogurt and casino slots. My ritual when operating a turn to LAS became work my butt off, walk into the airport, buy a frozen yogurt, eat that frozen yogurt while walking towards the casino slots, try my luck using one quarter (I'm not much of a gambler), lose, return to the aircraft, work by butt off again, go home. One of those days my loss had turned into a win, and I had gone home with over $100 extra. I was with a colleague of mine, who also enjoyed the LAS frozen yogurt, so once all the passengers had disembarked and the groomers had arrived, she and I went into the airport together. With our delicious treats in hand, I asked her if she didn't mind walking through the slots area with me so I could drop in a single quarter—my tradition there. There were only a few rows of slots and a handful of people playing, so it was rather quiet, which made my win seem even louder than expected. I dropped in my quarter, and the machine started singing and spitting coins back out at me.

"I won!" I exclaimed, as if my friend, who had been with me the whole time, didn't already know.

She looked at her watch. "We have to go," she said. "Boarding is going to start soon."

"I'm not leaving without my money," I told her, "but you go on ahead. Tell the flight director I'm coming."

She agreed and left probably wishing she had also played, while I collected my winnings. Once I had every last quarter in the coin bucket, I went to exchange it for bills. (Walking back to the aircraft with a bucket of quarters would have been awkward.) I still managed to make it back before boarding had even started. I guess it was just my lucky day.

The services provided on turns have changed quite drastically over the years. When I first started, even on a short two-and-a-half-hour flight, we would provide a complimentary hot meal service accompanied by wine in economy. At one point, we even served ice cream as a snack. This didn't last long, however, for two reasons: it got too messy the second the ice cream started melting, and the flight attendants ate way too many of them themselves. Eventually it turned into more meal and drink options but at a cost, and so BOB* (or buy on board) became the norm on turns.

I usually tried to avoid deadheads because this meant I was on duty but not getting full pay. Deadheading could mean flying as a passenger on my own airline, a different airline, by bus, or by train. I figured if I was going to be flying with my own airline anyway, I might as well work and make more money. I much preferred standing and walking around even if I had to work rather than simply sitting at my seat for hours on end. This would be especially true if it was a bumpy flight and I was feeling nauseous.

On one of my deadheads, I was seated next to a little girl and her mother, and I knew I was going to be sick, but I didn't want to use the airsickness bag right there next to them. The second the seat-belt sign went off on landing, I made a mad dash for the lavatory in the front galley only to find the flight director's crew bag in there. As there was no time to spare, I straddled his bag and did what I had to do while hoping for no back splash from the toilet. I felt relieved; although the flight director, who was now examining his bag for vomit remnants after my profuse apology, did not.

If I operated a flight immediately after a deadhead, it made sense to already be dressed in uniform, but this sometimes meant that passengers would look at me and think I was being lazy. It was easier to be inconspicuous if I was seated next to a window, so I would try to request this instead of an aisle seat, but it wasn't always available. I remember another deadhead when I was in my seat trying to "hide" as best I could by scooching down low in my seat and reading a magazine, when a passenger stood in the aisle next to me and asked if I could get him a drink. "Sorry, I'm not working," I told him and directed him towards the back galley. Usually if multiple crew members were deadheading together, the company would try to seat them with one another, but when I was on my own, I found I would have to explain to at least one person why I was in uniform but not currently working. If given the choice, the best option when having to deadhead on a turn (in other words, to travel as a passenger on a flight that leaves and returns the same day) was to do so on the return leg* (portion). This way I could get changed and blend in with the regular passengers. If the deadhead was with a different airline after operating on our own flight, some crew would choose to get changed, while others remained in their uniform. Even though remaining in uniform on a different airline usually meant getting "judged" by their crew members, I still tended to take this option because these types of deadheads were typically after an overseas in-flight, which meant I stunk and didn't want to contaminate my limited supply of clothes—besides, it was quicker to get through customs as crew. By judged I mean what all air crew inevitably do—they would check out our uniform and either favourably compare us to their own or mock us like a bunch of high schoolers.

Deadheading on another airline came with some challenges at times, especially after already operating a flight. Delays and cancellations could mean having to wait around in the airport much longer than anticipated for the next available flight. The pristine look we might have started off with had since departed by this point. Different rules and regulations applied to the various airlines, and normally we were aware of them and knew what was expected, such as with no carry-ons or pre-selected seats; however, on one occasion, one of my colleagues was left behind due to our lack of information. She was pregnant at the time and had operated the flight over with us but was informed she could not fly on our deadhead carrier due to their stricter flying-while-pregnant rules. As much as she explained she was fine and had just worked the flight over, they still refused to let her on. She was put up in an airport hotel and sent back home on our own airline the next day while the rest of us carried on without her. Even though some flight attendants enjoyed deadheading, I always thought they were more trouble than they were worth.

Ferry flights,* on the other hand, were awesome. I would operate a ferry flight any time I could. On these flights, no passengers were on board, and we were paid our full amount. Unlike deadheading, *we* oversaw the operation of emergency doors in case anything happened, and with that, came full pay. The flights would be empty on the outbound because it would be the last flight of the season, and so we would only be bringing passengers back home, but sometimes it would also be empty on the inbound with it being the first flight out. The "worst" thing about a ferry flight, was trying to figure out where you wanted to sit and which movie you wanted to watch. I had a flight once in which it was supposed to be a ferry, but instead we ended up bringing one couple back home with us. An entire plane with a full crew for two people. They couldn't believe their luck and were completely ecstatic.

Direct flights were flights that took you from your point of origin to your destination on one aircraft; however, it did not mean that it would not make other stops along the way. A direct, non-stop flight was what you would need if you wanted to avoid any other stops. Some passengers would get confused by the terminology and would therefore be surprised when we would make a stop that they were unaware of. I used to try to avoid working these types of flights because there was always too much wasted time on the ground, in which I wouldn't be getting paid. The connecting flights were the non-direct flights where you would have to change planes to continue to your destination. Sometimes passengers would not give themselves enough leeway to get from one aircraft to their next one and thus cause themselves added stress. When I had to connect on multiple, different airlines on my trip to Africa with my family, I made sure we had plenty of time just in case. It was better being early and going for lunch or shopping in the airport rather than panicking to catch the next flight in time.

Travelling by confirmed or standby* were the options for crew and their selected family or friends who wanted to use their passes for discounted personal travel. Crew were also entitled to jump-seat privileges, though not their travelling companions. Even though standby travel was unlimited and allowed the opportunity to fly on other selected airlines as well, I found it to be much too stressful. It meant having to wait until check-in closed before possibly getting a seat on the aircraft. If that flight was the last one of the day, and it was your outbound, you could at least go home, but if it was your return flight and you didn't get on, it meant checking into *another* hotel and crossing your fingers that the next day would be better. Hopefully, you didn't have prior commitments at home and could afford to possibly be a few days late. Even if there was room on the flight by the time everyone had checked in, it still didn't mean that the seat was yours. If there were others travelling standby, it came down to a seniority/priority system.

My parents had an awful standby experience when they flew from Toronto to Paris with a stop in Montreal. When they boarded the aircraft in Toronto, it seemed there were plenty of seats and all would be fine, but once they landed in Montreal, things changed. New passengers boarded and my parents' seats were no longer available. Every seat had been sold out, and my parents had to check in to a hotel and try again the next day. The following day the flight was once again full, but this time it was because a pilot and his wife were also flying standby and bumped my parents out of the last two seats, since employees ranked higher in standby priority than family of employees. On their third day in Montreal my parents finally made it on but swore to never fly standby again. After their experience, if I did choose standby as a travel option, I made sure it was only for the outbound portion and I could confirm the return.

Confirmed passes were limited to four a year (as long as you worked the entire year prior), which meant we could reserve a seat with our own airline a few weeks in advance. Who you gave the four tickets to was limited to select family members or a travel companion as long as they were travelling with you. If you had a family of five (such as mine), you were given five confirmed passes, but they all had to be used together. If I only used one confirmed pass, for instance, then I would only have three left to use. Travel was obviously limited to where our airline flew, but it was much less stressful. Although confirmed passes were not standby flights and you knew in advance that you held a seat on your flight, they still did not guarantee that you would get on. If changes needed to happen to accommodate revenue passengers, then those with confirmed passes would be the first ones removed. I was once at the airport with my parents, who were waiting to be checked in for their confirmed flight to Venice, when a ground agent approached them. Apparently there had been an aircraft change and because the new aircraft held fewer seats, my parents were taken off the flight. Luckily, they were given the option of flying to Rome later that evening instead. As inconvenient as this was, it was still better than cancelling everything and going home, so I made a phone call to their car rental place to change the pickup location, and after a sob story, my parents were promised an upgraded luxury car once they arrived. Their drive would be longer, but at least it would be comfortable.

Jump seat travel meant requesting to sit in a jump seat on the plane. It was restricted to crew, and you had to be in uniform. The advantage to this was that if there were no cabin seats available, you still had a chance of getting on. When I vacationed in Italy with my family one year, I had brought my uniform along just in case I would have to request a jump seat on the return because we left before I could confirm our inbound. It was during a blackout period,* which had different rules, that I would never attempt again nor recommend to anyone. My eldest daughter ended up getting a confirmed seat two days before the rest of us because she had to go back to work, but because it was in club class, I had to pay extra. Two days later, my husband was given a seat on a flight to a different city, and then he used his travel points to fly the rest of the way home. On the same day as my husband's flight, my other two children managed to secure themselves the last two cabin seats on the aircraft going directly home. Those last two seats were in club class, however, so I once again had to pay extra for the upgrade. I was told I would be sitting in a jump seat and would therefore be required to remain in my uniform, but once boarding commenced I was able to change into my regular clothes because one seat had opened up in economy. Unfortunately, my husband had already left on his different flight by this time. Neither one of my selfish kids opted to switch seats with me, but being alone in my economy seat proved to be quite peaceful.

Red-eye flights were fittingly named that because by the time you landed, your eyes tended to be red from lack of sleep. These were usually the overseas flights because they left late at night and arrived early the next morning. I usually tried to avoid working these flights for obvious reasons. If you're unable to get any shut-eye on these flights, eye drops could at least offer some relief for those red irritated eyes.

Repatriation flights were specially added flights to bring passengers back to their home country who may have been stranded elsewhere. This could have been due to their airline abandoning them because of bankruptcy for instance or due to border closures, as was the case with the COVID-19 outbreak. Passengers were never demanding and always grateful just to get home on these flights. I volunteered to work on a scheduled vacation day to help on a repatriation flight during COVID because I felt sorry for the stranded passengers.

The last three flight distinctions that I had mentioned at the beginning of this chapter are ones that I had personally never flown on; however, I can briefly touch upon them from what I've seen and heard. The military flights were some of my colleagues' favourites because they were flights filled with military personnel who were extremely disciplined and not to mention easy on the eyes. No one ever questioned or argued with the flight attendants on these flights. They simply did what they were told in a well-mannered fashion. I'm still kicking myself for never having requested to work on these flights. The humanitarian flights were those in which airlines would send aid and supplies to places in need due to natural disasters, such was the case with Haiti in 2016, when it was badly hit by a hurricane. The charity flights were special flights in which children with critical illnesses were provided with free travel. This included a yearly event with my airline of the search-for-Santa flight to the North Pole. As much as I would have enjoyed volunteering in this last type of flight, I was a blubbering mess when it came to ill children, so I knew it was best if I left this to others.

Regardless of which type of flight I worked on, flying was always an adventure. The adventure was much more enjoyable on ferry flights and much less on standby flights, mind you. Ferry flights allowed this introverted flight attendant room to thrive. Whereas I just found standby flights too stressful, especially if I was travelling with others. No matter how many types of flights were available, flying was still something my mother-in-law absolutely refused to have any part in whatsoever. But she's weird, so don't listen to her.

*blackout period: Not as in the loss of memory experienced after excessive drinking or the loss of electrical power, but rather this term refers to the dates specified by an airline during which promotional or discounted travel is prohibited or restricted.

*BOB (buy on board): Not to be confused with BYOB, this can either be used to refer to the service in which passengers have the option of purchasing items on board or the actual handheld machine used to accept payments (also not to be confused with Bob the flight attendant).

*ferry flights: Not as in a boat to carry passengers short distances or flights full of fairies for those who don't know how to spell *fairy*, but rather these flights refer to aircraft without any passengers from one airport to another.

*leg: Not as in the limb used to walk, but rather a leg is the portion of a flight from one airport to another. A flight may have more than one leg if it has multiple stops (my ideal flights had two legs, one for outbound and one for inbound).

*standby: In this context this term refers to getting a last-minute seat on a flight without advance reservations; however, it is often heard among flight attendants when requesting someone to wait a minute and will often end up being used when speaking with family and friends as well.

Chapter Seven

The Specials

When someone was labelled as a "special" passenger on board, it did not mean that person was a VIP. Special passengers were travellers who had special needs, such as those in wheelchairs or with impairments, pets, unaccompanied minors; and babies. (Actual VIPs were referred to as VIPs.) We were always notified of any specials during the pre-flight briefing. These were the expected specials. It was the unexpected and wannabe specials who were usually the ones that rendered some of my flights quite challenging.

When travelling at 38,000 feet, sometimes situations would arise that were completely out of our control, and we dealt with them as best as we could with what limited resources we had. Aside from the all-too-common sinus problems or motion sickness, I had passengers requiring oxygen, having seizures, fainting, getting cut or burnt, experiencing a heart attack, hyperventilating, and other unexplained illnesses. These were the unexpected specials. And on top of these unexpected specials, we also had to deal with the wannabe specials, which included the drunk, the irate, the nervous, and the downright rude passengers.

The expected specials, such as our wheelchair passengers, hardly ever caused any issues. In fact, I'd say we were the ones who caused them grievances. For some reason, they were usually seated towards the rear of the aircraft. So, if they were capable of walking with assistance and not straight backs,* we would test their limits by seating them forty rows back. If an expected special was unable to walk, a small-sized wheelchair was used to transport the passenger down our tight aisles and into their seat. Flight attendants were not allowed to assist in this, as there were specifically trained ground personnel to carry out these duties. In the air, however, we had our own version of a narrow wheelchair that could be assembled and used to transport a passenger as needed. It was cumbersome, and thankfully I never had to use one. I would have much rather spent the entire flight assisting a passenger get to and from the lavatories than use this contraption. (I did, in fact, spend a good portion of a flight once helping an elderly woman make her way back and forth to the lavs, but I didn't mind because this meant my colleagues had to help with my regular services.) Upon landing, these passengers had to wait until all other passengers were off the aircraft before their wheelchair would be brought to the gate. Sometimes the entire crew would sit and chat with them because, depending on the required number of wheelchairs needed, this process could take quite long, and we were not allowed to leave until all the passengers had deplaned.

For the passengers who had a visual, hearing, or intellectual impairment, we were taught certain techniques that would assist in their safety and comfort. For someone visually impaired, for example, we would explain everything verbally while demonstrating the location of certain items. For the hearing impaired, we used gestures and spoke slowly and directly. And for those with an intellectual impairment, just speaking directly was usually sufficient. Aside from the passenger who told me off by way of hand gestures, I never had any issues with these specials. I did once witness a flight attendant speaking loudly to a blind passenger though. I think she was a little tired and confused.

I, too, had fumbled once, but I was six at the time. My father had to have a procedure performed on both of his eyes, which left him wearing bandages for the following few days. Being the kind and caring daughter that I was, I asked him what I could do to help. He told me he'd like to watch television, so I guided him over to the couch, helped him get seated, and asked which channel he'd like to watch. My dad was a jokester, and I had naively fallen for his shenanigans.

Next we had the pregnant and the overweight passengers. Please do not take offence to this. These groups simply faced the same challenges, and having been pregnant while flying, I, too, was familiar with the woes. The aisles on most of our planes were not designed for an average-to-large adult to walk through without having to side shuffle. I always knew when I had gained weight because my hips would be hitting the passengers sitting in the aisle seats. When I became pregnant, I could only walk sideways down the aisles. Extension seat belts were not an option when seated at an emergency exit, as they could potentially cause a tripping hazard during an emergency, and consequently, I was not allowed to sit in certain jump seats on board because the straps were too short. My manager asked me to meet her at the aircraft one morning and had me sit in every jump seat to test where I would fit (not all jump seat straps were the same length). If these passengers were not seated in an emergency row, I would gladly give them an extension seat belt on request. Just like I would never ask a stranger if she was pregnant, I would never ask passengers if they required an extension seat belt. There was, however, an upside to working while pregnant—I could milk it. Many passengers would feel sorry for me and would even offer to help me with my services. Just like being able to get away with saying, "But I'm eating for two now," I enjoyed it while I could.

My Fur Baby IG @bellotheyorkie

By far my favourite special passengers were of the furry nature—the dogs. They were either used for service, emotional support, or if small enough, as part of someone's carry-on luggage. The cats were cute too, but I had a severe cat allergy, so I never fared well when these felines were on board. The only rules with dogs were that their extremities did not protrude into the aisles, and they remained on leash and wore a vest or a harness. If in a carrier, they needed to remain in that carrier, and if not, they had to remain at the passenger's feet or stay on a lap. I may have been a little more friendly and lenient towards passengers with pets. What can I say? I'm a sucker for animals.

The unaccompanied minors (UMs) were my next favourite specials. They were children ages eight to eleven who were travelling alone. I found that most children behaved much better alone than they normally would when around their family or friends. For the most part, the UMs listened and were easygoing. If we had more than one on board, we would try to seat them together. I'm pretty sure I treated them better than my own children. To be fair, though, the UMs never talked back or told me I embarrassed them. I remember one specific UM who was so polite and well-travelled that I wanted to take him home with me. He was ten years old and going to visit his grandparents in Florida. He had already been to so many interesting places in the world that he put me to shame. Plus, he never forgot to say please or thank you, and he called me miss instead of ma'am (bonus points).

We always had to be aware of any babies on board because they (meaning their parents) required a special briefing during boarding. Infants were classified as such up until the age of two. They did not require a seat and therefore did not wear a seat belt. If the parent chose to purchase a seat, the baby could sit in an approved car seat; otherwise, they were considered lapheld. Anytime there was any issue involving a baby, it was either due to the parents themselves or the baby-hating passengers. If seated in a bulkhead seat, parents of an infant could request an airplane bassinet. This was a detachable cot to rest the baby in during the flight. If that baby met the height and weight restrictions and the detachable cot was not used anytime the seat-belt sign was on, there would not have been any problems. And yet issues would still arise because many passengers refused to take their babies out during turbulence for fear of waking them, or they would use the bassinet to store all their belongings while the baby slept on the floor, or the parents would blatantly lie about their baby's weight and then get upset when further questioned. Despite the annoyances and inconveniences that these interactions would sometimes create, because these parents of babies and the other "expected" passengers were, in fact, expected, I found it a lot easier to mentally prepare for dealing with them. It was the unexpecteds who often threw me and my colleagues for a curve ball.

The unexpected, special passengers were those who were not mentioned during our pre-flight briefing because they were, quite frankly, a surprise to everyone. These were the passengers who would develop medical conditions or illnesses while in the air. It could be something as serious as a heart attack or as simple as a nosebleed. I did not sympathize with the idiotic passengers who chose to ignore the laws and regulations and risked jeopardizing others' safety; however, I *did* feel sorry for passengers in a medical emergency. Like the passenger who had been seated directly in front of my jump seat as we were preparing to land and whose eyes rolled backwards just before his body went into convulsions. Since all I could do was ensure the area around him didn't cause him any injuries, I felt helpless. It was as if the plane was set on mute mode because either no one spoke, or I was so focused on this poor passenger that my mind went into tunnel vision and only saw and heard him. Once we landed, the paramedics boarded, and he was carried off the aircraft. I never found out anything more about his condition; although, he was at least conscious when he left.

I'll also never forget the time an elderly gentleman had safely disembarked our return flight home only to have a heart attack on the escalator and end up lying upside down on the now motionless stairs while slowly turning blue. His body was lying in a 180-degree angle of the upward escalator with his head closest to the bottom steps. Someone had stopped the escalator before we had arrived. The crew and I attempted to help, but luckily the paramedics arrived quickly and were able to take over.

These were the proud moments I recalled with fondness of everyone working together. These were the times I still *liked* people. I was thankful to be able to say that during all my years of flying no one had ever passed away while on board one of my flights. Unfortunately, I have heard the tragic stories from other flight attendants that, despite the crew's best efforts, one of their passengers didn't survive. The only thing left they could do was console their loved one.

Most of the medical situations I encountered were fortunately minor and easily resolved. Sinus problems were extremely common and the cause of most babies' crying upon landing. Taking a decongestant before flying, and possibly again before landing depending on the length of the flight, was an easy fix. Whenever I flew anywhere with my children, my husband and I would dose them up with decongestant (the drowsy kind), just to be on the safe side. Once descent had commenced, some people preferred to use hot compresses, either directly behind the ears or by placing the steeped cloth in a cup and covering the ears with steam. Gum chewing or yawning also seemed to work for some. As for babies, suckling was sometimes enough to do the trick. I once had to take a leave of absence from work due to fluid in my ear caused by flying with a cold. It felt like my head was underwater. It took about two weeks before I was able to properly hear again. The lesson learned was to not fly sick. And it was not a good idea to fly the day after a root canal either. Trust me. I was in extreme pain for the entire duration of the flight after a routine root canal. You might also want to give yourself at least a day before flying if you've been scuba diving, as this can lead to decompression sickness.

Aside from sinus problems, motion sickness was also quite common and was a condition I could completely relate to. I had to deal with my own motion sickness much more than that of passengers when I initially started working as a flight attendant. Ever since I could remember I suffered from motion sickness, particularly in the mornings for some reason. In fact, my mother had to switch me from morning to afternoon kindergarten classes because I couldn't even endure the short, early-morning bus rides. Flying was hands down the worst for me. When I was fifteen years old, I was returning on a flight from Europe with my mother, and I swore to her I would never fly again. This was after having vomitted for the gazillionth time, and I was crying because everything hurt by that point. The poor man sitting near me couldn't even stomach his meal anymore. In retrospect, I had done him a favour because who enjoyed airline food anyway? Who would have ever imagined that roughly eight years later, I would be part of a flight crew?

I had always had the tendency of acting before thinking, so when I was hired as a flight attendant, I hadn't put much thought into the fact that motion sickness always got the better of me. It wasn't until I was physically sitting in the jump seat of my very first flight as a paid employee, stomach churning, thinking to myself, *Oh no, what did I do? Hold it together.* I started to sweat. The seat-belt sign turned off, and I made a mad dash for the lavatory. I had saved myself the humiliation of throwing up in front of everyone on my first day of work, but I knew it was going to be a *long* day.

The day I rode public transit with my mother, however, was when I hadn't been able to "hold it together." We were pulling into the subway station on a jam-packed bus when I just couldn't contain myself any longer. I had already been on the bus for about half an hour trying not to think of the usual motion sickness I was experiencing. All I could think when the bus rounded the corner into the station was, *Dear lord, please don't let me barf all over these poor people.* God did not listen. I took down three people with my vomit. They were disgusted, and I was mortified yet ironically relieved at the same time. A few minutes later in the ladies' bathroom, I ran into one of my victims, who was still trying to clean my contribution to her dress off her. She bolted out of the bathroom as soon as she saw it was me.

I tried motion sickness pills, the pressure bracelet, and the back-of-the-ear patch but all with no resolve. Time is all it would take to help. Over time my mad dashes occurred less and less. On one of my flights, however, we were having particularly stubborn turbulence. I thought I was handling it fairly well until right there, in the middle of my bar service, something was coming up with a vengeance. I ditched my trolley in the middle of the aisle and ran! Luckily, another flight attendant was able to quickly step in for me while I composed myself. A few minutes later, as I stood leaning up against the forward galley counter, my flight director ever so motherly said to me, "Maybe this isn't the right profession for you." I felt so defeated but I was no quitter. Besides, I was stubborn, so I *needed* to win this battle with motion sickness.

If there was one thing I knew a lot about, it was vomit. This proved to be helpful over the years, since there was at least one vomitter on every flight. Even though air sickness pills did not work for me, there were many who swore by them. The problem I had with them was that they didn't prevent me from feeling nauseous but rather only prevented me from vomiting. I preferred even the temporary feeling of relief rather than the continuous feeling of nausea. Flat ginger ale proved to work best for me, and it's what I would suggest to my passengers as well. Vomit happened—there was no need to be embarrassed, but it would be helpful if passengers could be considerate with their aim. What I learned over the years was that there were four types of vomitters. There were the projectile vomitters, the dry heavers, the repeat offenders, and the popular hacking-your-brains-out vomitters. Regardless of which one you were, if you knew you experienced motion sickness, prepare yourself with not only enough air sickness bags but also at least one plastic bag, antiseptic wipes, and a toothbrush and toothpaste—or at the very least, some breath mints. For smaller children, you might want to bring a change of clothes. The change of clothes idea wouldn't hurt for adults as well. I once had an elderly gentleman on one of my flights who, after four bouts of vomitting, ended up wearing nothing but two of our blankets off the plane.

In most cases, there was at least one doctor or nurse on board who thankfully was willing to help with the unexpected medical situations. I recall one of my flights where it seemed like everything was running smoothly. I even had a chance to sit down and grab a bite, which tended to be rare on a turn. The moment I settled in with my meal, however, the passenger standing in the aisle next to me waiting to use the lavatory simply fainted. One minute she was standing, and next thing I knew she was passed out on the floor. I quickly finished my meal and proceeded to help. Okay, fine, I didn't finish my meal, but I did toy with the idea for a few solid seconds, since the sight of someone fainting did not faze me anymore—it had become such a common occurrence on board my flights.

Another time I was cleaning up my beverage trolley in the galley when a woman standing near me warned me that she was going to faint. Not a second later, she was going down. Luckily, the half-second warning she gave me was enough for me to be able to catch her and gently lower her to the ground, thanks to my lightning-fast reflexes. These were the simple cases in which a wet compress on the back of the neck or forehead and elevated legs was all that was needed.

Administering oxygen was also quite common. Sometimes a little O_2 was all it took to calm someone down. I had an elderly woman once who told me she was claustrophobic and asked it if I could open the window just a crack. Trying not to laugh at the passengers proved to be challenging at times. Then there were others who would get themselves very worked up about flying, to the point of panic, particularly during the critical phases of turbulence, take-offs, and landings. I witnessed passengers crying, praying, and clawing their nails into their armrests or into their partner's arms. Some tried to hide their fears by drinking, which tended to cause a whole slew of other problems. This brought us to the wannabe passengers.

The wannabes were just that. They were neither expected nor unexpected and wanted in on the "action." The most common wannabes were the intoxicated. Drinking didn't even have to start on the plane before it was already a problem. Many times, we found ourselves waiting for latecomers who were coming from the airport bars trying to get in that last drink before boarding. Someone who appeared intoxicated at boarding, however, might be denied since this was a violation of regulations. I vividly remembered watching a passenger stagger down the aisle during a final boarding call and attempt to take his seat. He had somehow managed to fake soberness on his way past both the check-in agent and the flight attendant at the boarding door. Just as I was about to cross the aisle to approach him to confirm my suspicions, he projectile vomitted. As the star flight attendant I was, I retreated back to my section pretending not to have noticed. He was ultimately escorted off the flight, and the groomers were called back on for a quick cleanup.

On another occasion, I was returning from an overseas flight and oversaw boarding. Besides greeting the passengers and giving them directions to their seats, I also had to be aware of passenger baggage and behaviour, which could potentially cause a problem in flight. Asking to see the boarding cards was not only to guide passengers in the right seat direction but also to ensure they were on the right aircraft and, in fact, going to the correct destination. Usually this was discovered while still on the ground, but I did have a flight in which the passenger came all the way with us to a different city without anyone realizing. There were two flights with my airline leaving from Punta Cana at roughly the same time, except one was going to Montreal and the other to Toronto with me. At least our Montreal-bound passenger didn't stray too far from home. The seat he was assigned was coincidentally vacant, and those who checked his boarding card (not me) hadn't realized it was a different airport code. The poor bugger only became aware once we were landing and the flight director made her welcome announcement. I didn't know how or when the passenger returned to Montreal, but I was sure he was taken care of by our lovely ground crew—although he didn't look too happy when I passed him on the bridge where he was arguing with an agent.

At any rate, back to my overseas boarding story. I had asked a passenger to see his boarding card, and instead, he rifled through his murse (man purse) and pulled out a wad of cash. I could smell the alcohol coming off him as he swayed back and forth waving the money in my face, as if to pay me off. I told him that wouldn't do and proceeded to call my flight director over. He was clearly intoxicated, and I knew all too well what having an intoxicated passenger on board would be like if he was allowed on. Even the ones who tended to eventually fall asleep first felt it necessary to cause a disturbance of sorts. I continued with my boarding, as the flight director, captain, and ground agent were now dealing with this person. He was consequently deemed unfit to fly, and we left him behind. He was clearly upset and still arguing with the ground agent on the bridge when I closed the door. On a positive note, I knew he had enough cash to get by.

What many people didn't realize was that the same amount of alcohol doubled its effect once in the air. Basically the low oxygen levels in the blood would render that same passenger wobblier than when on the ground. When I was able to acquire enough seniority to pick and choose my destinations, I would always opt for morning turns instead of those departing in the afternoon primarily because of the amount of alcohol the passengers would drink. On the morning flights, the passengers tended to be too tired still and would fall asleep on take-off. (This did not apply to the flights to Newfoundland, though, in which we would run out of beer during our breakfast service.) On the afternoon and evening flights, our passengers were ready to party even before arriving at their all-inclusive resorts. The worst were the spring break yahoos because they were among their friends and ready for some wilding. Much like dogs, teenagers could sense if you feared them, and so you had to show them who was in charge right from the get-go. Whenever I was stuck working these flights, I made sure any unaccompanied teenager in my section had their ID at the ready. In fact, one of my colleagues found it quite comical when she heard me speaking to an entire section warning them that if they wanted any alcohol, they would need to produce their passports. And, like good little soldiers listening to their sergeant, everyone had taken out their passports and placed them on their tray table. (Insert mic drop.)

There were certain tactics that we could use as flight attendants to deter someone from getting drunk. This included slowing down the rate of service to that passenger so that they weren't getting too many drinks too quickly. To ensure this was effective, the rest of the crew had to be made aware of the situation, as that passenger would inevitably attempt to ask multiple flight attendants for drinks as well. Another method was to also give them water with their drink to at least help with the diuretic effect of drinking alcohol. Ultimately, we could cut that passenger off from drinking completely, if necessary. The maximum we were permitted to give to a passenger at once was two drinks; however, this didn't stop some from getting creative and asking others to purchase drinks for them.

Then there were those who would only ask for a cup of ice. These were the sneaky ones who were secretly drinking their own large bottles of alcohol from duty-free. (Ironically, we were the ones who had told them during boarding that they needed to place any duty-free bottles under the seat in front of them and not in the overhead bin.) I'm not saying that everyone who requested only ice was drinking their own stash, but we made sure to keep a closer eye on them, just in case. Even those sweet old grandmas could not be trusted.

I once had an annoyingly long conversation with a passenger as to why he couldn't drink his own alcohol on board. He was an older gentleman travelling back from Italy on his own, sitting in an aisle seat. When we were preparing the cabin to land, I noticed he didn't store his backpack away but instead, kept it standing open on his lap.

"Sir, I'm going to need you to place your bag under the seat for landing," I told him and walked away thinking he would follow directions.

When I looked back to ensure the bag was now off his lap, I instead saw that he appeared to be drinking from a bottle he had pulled out of it. I immediately walked back to him just as he was placing the bottle of whiskey back into his bag. "Sir, you cannot drink your own alcohol on board."

He looked at me all confused. *"Non capisco,"* he responded, claiming in Italian that he didn't understand.

So I proceeded to repeat what I had just told him, but in Italian this time. His confused look turned to that of someone who had been wrongfully accused, and he became immediately defensive. (For simplicity's sake, the rest of our dialogue was translated into English.)

"What's the problem?" he asked. "I didn't do anything wrong. I bought this in the airport duty-free boutique."

He believed because the bottle didn't come from home but rather was purchased in duty-free, it counted as being purchased from the airline. "No, sir, it doesn't work that way," I told him. I proceeded to let him know that regulations stated a passenger could not drink their own alcohol unless it was served by a flight attendant on board. He wasn't having it.

"No, you're wrong," he said. "I have every right to drink this."

"Then why were you trying to hide it?" I rebutted. By this point one of the other flight attendants had noticed our little confrontation and had already taken it upon herself to call the flight director for backup. When she arrived, she asked me to translate for her as she further explained the regulations. The rules were in place to help control passengers' consumption to prevent intoxication. When a passenger was discovered drinking their own alcohol, they not only had their bottle confiscated but were met by the authorities on landing, who were always more than happy to remind them of the regulations as well as possibly serve them with a hefty fine.

As much as I tried to explain all this to the passenger, he was just not letting up. "I'll need your bottle and passport," I said on behalf of the flight director. Grudgingly, he gave in and tossed them to us. He sulked in his seat while I informed him that he'd need to stay behind when we landed. Once all the passengers had disembarked, he was left in the hands of the ground crew and the authorities. My job had been done and I was free to leave.

Unfortunately, as much as we tried to prevent drunkenness on board, it was still a quite common occurrence. When I first started with the airline, we accepted cash, so I used to have to carry around my own float to make change for our passengers. On one of my flights, I was in the middle of my beverage service and had given an alcoholic drink to a young lady, but I didn't have exact change for her at the moment, so I told her I'd be back with her change as soon as I had it. She was fine with that, and I proceeded with the service.

Not more than five minutes later this same passenger came barrelling up the aisle towards me screaming obscenities. Something about flight attendants and pigs and how I ripped her off. "Where's my fucking money, you mother fuckin' bunch of fuckin' no good pigs!?" (or something to that nature) she screamed as she attempted to punch me, but, luckily for me, the beverage trolley stood between us. I stood there in shock. Maybe this was just a *really* bad dream. "You guys are all fucking assholes!" she continued and stormed up the aisle once she had failed to reach me.

Passengers looked just as puzzled and concerned as I did, but no one wanted to intervene. That day, there just so happened to be a very tall and intimidating flight attendant working in the club class section. When he heard the commotion, he came rushing to my aid along with the flight director. "Get back to your seat!" my colleague (hero) ordered her. Together he and the flight director managed to calm the passenger down by ways of threats, while I, finally relieved, was able to breathe again. Her passport was then confiscated, the authorities notified, and she was obviously cut off from any further alcohol. She ended up sleeping for the rest of the flight. Upon landing, the authorities were already at the gate awaiting our arrival. It was discovered that she was on medication that had adverse effects when mixed with alcohol. I still owe her change to this day.

Not all my passengers were as appeasing, though. Some of the irate were verbally as well as physically abusive. I couldn't tell you the number of times I' was told to fuck off by a passenger. One of the flight directors I worked with actually had to go on short-term disability after he was punched by an intoxicated passenger. (Too bad he didn't have a beverage trolley to protect him like I did.) Sometimes even the tiniest thing could set someone off. When I first started flying, I would work on an aircraft in which we stored our cups in an overhead bin closest to the front galley. When I opened the bin to retrieve a sleeve of cups, one of them was loose and fell onto the passenger's legs seated directly under.

"Ow!" he yelled as he grabbed his knee, as if he had just been beaten by a bat.

"Oh, I'm sorry," I said to him apologetically, but not genuinely so because it was just a plastic cup after all.

"I'm going to sue this company!" he threatened as he continued to hug his knee and wince in pain.

I couldn't believe what I was witnessing. One small plastic cup had touched his leg before landing on the floor, and he was pretending to be in agony. I wanted to tell him he would do great during our training scenarios in the plane simulator but thought best to just bite my tongue and offer him a free drink as a peace offering instead. Funny enough the alcohol served as a medicinal aid, and his knee magically recovered. This would be just the beginning of a career full of crazies.

The good thing about flight attendants was they tended to be strong and resilient. I was not the type to harbour resentment, and the moment I stepped off the plane, I left any stresses of the day behind. The longer you worked as a flight attendant, the easier it was to just let things roll off your shoulders, even the unruly and demanding passengers.

I could usually spot problem passengers before we had even taken off because they would be the ones who thought it was extremely inconvenient to show their boarding card, complained about their seat, complained about their overhead bin space, and continued to talk on their cell phone even after being asked on several occasions to turn it off. These were the same passengers who believed I was there to serve them and them alone. They loved monopolizing my time. I had a passenger once ream me out during boarding because he didn't believe he should have to place his duty-free bottles under the seat in front of him. I tried to explain to him that for safety measures, they could not be stored in the overhead bins.

Passengers had a tendency of releasing their frustrations and stresses out on flight attendants, even when out of our control. And in this case, there was no pleasing him. As far as he was concerned, he knew better, and I was wrong.

"I have been flying for over twenty years and have never heard of this rule in my life," he said to me.

I tried to explain that because his bottles were simply in a plastic bag, they could slide around and break if placed in the overhead bin. He continued to tell me I was being ignorant. Then I slapped him. Psych! Just making sure you were paying attention. I *wanted* to slap him, but instead, as much as it pained me, I let him finish his rant. When I turned my back momentarily to let a passenger pass (since we were still boarding), he felt insulted.

"So now you're going to ignore me?!" he yelled. How dare I did not give him my complete, undivided attention and let others board the aircraft.

"Sir, I was just letting others pass so we can take off," I explained.

His rant caused the passenger seated behind him to finally intervene. He did not appreciate the attitude of this irate passenger and how he was speaking to me, particularly in front of his small children. "Sir, you need to stop. I have kids here. You're being ridiculous and rude. An announcement was even made about bottles going under the seat. If you had stopped arguing for one minute, you would have heard it." he said to him over the seat.

This passenger then turned to me and asked, "Can I get your name? I'd like to write a comment card on your behalf."

This simple gesture by another passenger was all that was needed to put my problem passenger in his place and silence him. Guess which passenger got a free beer during the flight?

Then there were the baby haters who believed everyone else on board should be a baby hater as well, and how dare we have any crying babies on board. The nerve. Complaining over something so petty was not uncommon behaviour for the wannabes. Babies cried. It was what they did. They ate, slept, pooped, and cried. I was not sure what they wanted me to do about this. I usually felt sympathetic towards the parents of the crying baby, who would be attempting to do anything they could to soothe their child. It was not like they were encouraging their baby to cry just to spite everyone. When a baby was inconsolable, I found it was usually due to ear pain during take-off and landing, since a baby's ears couldn't adjust to the pressure like an adult's ears could. If I had the choice between a plane full of babies and a plane full of adults, the former would win hands down. I was used to baby and children noises from being a mom, so what others might have found irritating, I could easily block out. It was the irrational or drunk adults I couldn't block out. So yes, I'd take an Orlando flight any day.

There were certain routes that were notorious for being problematic. I'd rather not give any specifics, but let's just say that fellow flight attendants would all agree. These routes included travelling to the Caribbean and overseas. As much as I tried to avoid these routes, sometimes it was inevitable. It was on these flights that I'd be told to fuck off when requesting someone to put their seat belt on. It was also the first time I had ever been *told* off by a deaf passenger. I had no idea what was happening when I saw his hands frantically gesturing, until he flipped me the bird. Got it.

There were also certain rules and regulations that passengers repeatedly challenged, which made patience a definite must as a flight attendant. I had to be able to pick my battles, be flexible, and adapt to change as required. The seat-belt sign was illuminated, the announcement to buckle up had been made and I had given a friendly reminder. Aside from personally sitting on the passengers, whether they chose to wear their seat belt or not was now out of my hands.

The ban on smoking was another regulation that many continued to challenge. Not only did they attempt to smoke in the lavatories, but some also did not even try to conceal it and simply lit up at their seat. It was still something that passengers did to this day, even though most were aware that the fine could be anywhere up to $5,000 under Canadian law as well as possible jail time or community service. Typically, the fine was around $500, but it was all dependent on the degree of damage or disruption the smoker caused. For example, the smoke detector in the lavatory might have been tampered with or the plane might have had to divert and land elsewhere due to a potential fire hazard. Our main priorities in these cases were where the cigarette butts were put out. They needed to be disposed of safely in case of fire. A fire in the air could be catastrophic. Without quick and proper intervention, it could take a plane down within minutes. Once that was in order, then we could continue to reprimand the guilty passenger, and, as in the other cases with disruptive or law-breaking passengers, they would be met by the authorities on landing.

When the flight directors would run through all the specials during our pre-flight briefing, in the back of my mind I always knew there would be way more on our flight than those listed, especially if it was a full moon. I knew besides the expected classification of passengers, there would also be two more—the unexpecteds and the wannabes. A full moon meant the wannabe specials were usually out in full force. Sometimes, however, we would even end up with fewer than expected specials by the end of the flight because the passengers who required a wheelchair upon boarding would run off the plane once we landed, leaving their reserved chair behind. Apparently even miracles were performed in the sky.

straight backs: Not as in rows of hair being braided flat to the scalp from the front to the back of the head or as in people with a straight back, but rather this term refers to passengers who are unable to walk.

Chapter Eight

The Customs Hall

When travelling internationally, going through customs was inevitable. As inconvenient and time consuming as it was, I knew it came with the job. Often passengers would ask whether I had to go through customs every time I returned home from work, and the answer was always a resounding yes, if I exited the country. Even though there were designated lines for crew members, sometimes these lines could get awfully long, and the last thing I'd want to do after a long day was stand in line and wait.

As much fun as I might have just had with my flight crew, once I stepped foot on that bridge it was a quick goodbye and a mad dash towards the customs hall. If I spotted another crew headed in the same direction, then the dash would become a full-out sprint. This was especially true when it was a crew of around twenty. There was no way I was going to stand behind all of them if I could help it. One time when I ended up getting caught in line between a different crew (so that a few of their members were in front of me and a few were behind), one of their flight attendants from behind asked if they could go ahead so they could be with the rest of their crew. *That's funny,* I thought. My reply (with a smile) was, "No, but your colleagues in front are welcome to join you behind me." Everyone ended up staying exactly where they were in line.

And then there were the people who used their "VIP status" to bypass the unwritten rules of customs lineups. I was a huge believer in treating everyone as equals, so if a VIP were to use their status to cut in line over an economy passenger or a flight attendant, for instance, I'd be peeved. Which is exactly how I felt the only time I'd ever spotted a true celebrity (I say true because that guy that everyone seems to know who works at the coffee shop doesn't count) while standing in the crew line at customs. It was that curly haired guy from some zombie movie. The only reason I had spotted him was because he was not in a flight crew uniform, and it had annoyed me that someone was being escorted through "my" line who wasn't even part of a flight crew. *How dare he!* I had just finished working a ten-hour overseas flight, and now this guy was taking up room in *my* line! *Back of the regular-folks line, bucko!* Maybe part of the reason why I was so oblivious to celebrities was that I myself was in my own zombie state after a flight. I was tired, hungry, and grouchy. *Patrick Stewart, who?* That was a lie. My family knew I loved Sir Stewart. I'd let him cut in front but no one else.

Sometimes when I would finally arrive at customs, I would be so tired that I couldn't even remember where I had just flown in from. When asked by the customs agent, it would not be uncommon for me to answer with a puzzled "uh . . . ," before having to turn to my colleagues still in line for the answer. Sometimes I could only remember the flight number, and the customs agent would then roll his eyes because I had inconvenienced his into now having to look it up. I'd be asked a few more questions, this time pertaining to any purchases made. Next, the agent would scribble on my customs declaration card, and I was permitted to pass through to the next checkpoint before heading into the baggage hall.

A colleague of mine was returning from a turnaround flight and was so extremely tired that when the customs agent asked about her flight, she mistook his question for a statement, so instead of simply answering, "Yes, it was a turnaround," she proceeded to raise her hands and slowly turn around in the form of a circle. I could just picture the customs agent shaking his head in disbelief. Customs agents probably thought of flight crew like the crew thought of passengers, except they didn't ever smile.

For the most part, one couldn't joke with customs agents, so when one of them asked me if I wanted a kiss one day, I just stood there in silence staring blankly. *What is the right answer? What do I say? Maybe if I pretend like I didn't hear him I could just move on.* Luckily, the agent only let me sweat for a few seconds before passing me a Hershey's Kiss chocolate.

After being interrogated at customs, I had to wave my declaration card at the next checkpoint agent, and then if the mark scribbled by the earlier agent on that card was deemed acceptable, I was able to continue and claim my luggage at the baggage hall—hopefully. If I could avoid it, I always tried not to bring any checked luggage with me. It was bad enough having to wait in line at customs, but then to have to further wait for my bag to arrive would just add insult to injury. As a flight crew member, I was entitled to baggage priority, which meant my bag was supposed to get pulled off the plane and placed onto the conveyor belt first before the passengers' luggage from that same flight. This wasn't always the case, however, as there were times when I had to wait for over an hour. Once I finally did have my checked luggage in hand, I now had to enter yet another line and surrender my declaration card to the third customs agent. This time the agent would simply take a visual scan of my card, and depending on what the first agent had scribbled on it, I was either directed to the exit or to the secondary hall for further inspection.

Walking towards the secondary hall was always daunting. I knew not to ever lie on the customs declaration form, so I would always declare everything; however, this didn't mean I was home free. Sometimes it was a random spot check for the entire crew. These were the annoying times when all I wanted to do was go home, but instead I had to grin and bear it because, otherwise, I could end up staying there even longer. They would rummage through my belongings, ask some questions, and once satisfied that everything was in order, I was permitted to make my final exit. Other times I knew that I'd be sent into secondary because of something I had brought back with me. (Being sent into secondary is an expression commonly used by flight attendants passing through customs.) Like the spring I bought tulip bulbs from Amsterdam as end-of-year teacher gifts for my children's teachers. Even though I had made sure they had the proper sticker of approval on them, I knew customs would still want to have them inspected. I was eventually fine and good to go. Once at this check point, though, there was no point in playing dumb. You had to admit what you had because the officers had heard and seen it all. (If you've seen *Border Security* on television, you can relate.) Even sweet, old grandma was not exempt.

On most occasions when I was travelling to the United States, I had to pre-clear customs. This meant going through American customs *before* going on the flight instead of after arriving. As it turned out, I became a regular in their secondary customs hall. Apparently, someone by my name living in the States was not a particularly good citizen, and so every time I passed through their customs, I was flagged and would then get interrogated on my whereabouts and intentions. It would become even more awkward when I'd run into passengers on my flight also waiting to be interrogated. It felt like back in grade school when you were sent down to the principal's office and had to wait in the waiting room with all the other delinquents.

One day I was finally fed up and asked one of the officers what I could do to avoid having to be interrogated every time. The solution was to join Nexus. It sounded like a cult, but essentially it was a program between Canada and the United States that allowed pre-approved travellers quicker and easier entry by use of automated, self-serve kiosks and dedicated lanes. *Perfect. Sign me up!*

I figured since I was going to apply for Nexus, I might as well sign my whole family up as well; that way when we were travelling together, it would be easier for all of us, and I wouldn't have to wait for them. The application process started with online forms and eventually led to an in-person interview. My family and I were all interviewed together because the children were still minors. My eldest daughter refused to listen to me when I told her not to wear her contacts, only to be later asked by the officer taking her eye retinal scan to remove them. My other daughter kept fussing with her hair trying to make sure it was in perfect order before getting her picture taken, only to later discover the picture was a close-up of only her face. When my son was asked if he was ever in trouble with the law, he responded that his teacher sent him down for detention once. Why did I sign my family up again? Nexus proved to be quite helpful in bypassing long lines and avoiding the secondary hall in U.S. customs as well as easier for travelling with my family, so I guess it had been worth a bit of humiliation during the interview.

As inconvenient and time consuming as going through customs was, especially when you were returning from a long flight and all you wanted to do was go home, it was an inevitable part of international travel. So, suck it up buttercup. But don't let a VIP cut in front of you, don't try to make the customs agent smile, do get yourself a Nexus pass (actually don't because then you'll make my line longer), and for heaven's sake, don't lie.

The Peeves

The peeves did not refer to that poltergeist character from *Harry Potter*. They were annoyances that people found irritating, otherwise known as pet peeves. I removed the word *pet* because that would reduce the significance to something cute or minor. Whether passengers were aware of these peeves was irrelevant, as they were nonetheless annoying. As a flight attendant for so many years, I had been privy to the many peeves of flying: ill-mannered passengers, unruly children and "blameless" parents, messy passengers, seat and baggage grievances, seat-belt unbuckling, and many other "little" annoyances worth sharing.

If there was one thing I'd learned, it was that patience was key as a flight attendant. This did not pertain just to airport lines, delays, or luggage issues but to the passengers and crew themselves. My patience was tested time and time again, and sometimes I would have to remind myself to just breathe. The peeves were annoying because they happened so frequently, and since they were common irritants, this meant they were not going to disappear anytime soon, and I would have to learn how to tolerate them or risk going all postal and popping a slide.*

The ill-mannered passengers outnumbered all the others. They were those who would forget to bring their manners with them when travelling. A lot could be said about a passenger in how they addressed or treated a flight attendant. First off, when speaking to a flight attendant, you needed to remove your headset or earbuds and make eye contact. I couldn't tell you how many times I'd asked a passenger what they'd like to drink, and, without even turning to face me, they replied, "What?" If I was still not acknowledged by the second attempt, I would move on. Sometimes I would get asked what we had to drink and after going through a well-recited list of items, that same passenger would then ask for something I hadn't mentioned at all. If you wanted something specific to drink, you had to ask for it first. This included when asking for coffee or tea—pretend you were at Starbucks—you needed to be specific with your order and not assume that I knew you took Splenda or preferred milk over cream. (Black coffee, by the way, did *not* have milk or creamer.) This brought me to my next point.

Besides the obvious niceties of saying please and thank you, when asking a flight attendant for a drink, if only a few minutes had passed, give that flight attendant the benefit of the doubt that he or she will return with said drink. If an hour has lapsed, you might want to then reorder. Repeating your order to multiple flight attendants could end up costing you an unnecessary trip to the lavatories, since we would bring you those multiples and death stare you into finishing them all—no one really liked to use the airplane lavatories if they didn't have to. As a side note, for all those passengers who I said, "Sure, no problem, be right back with your drink," but then never returned, I apologize. I assure you, however, that I would wake up in a panic in the middle of that night with the realization that I hadn't ever given you your glass of water.

We were flight attendants. Not waiters or waitresses, stewards or stewardesses, and most certainly not short-skirted sky sluts (hubby lingo). They did not answer to snapping of fingers or whistles. Although I knew a few who didn't mind the cat calls. Your best option was to press the call button or raise your hand. Calling out "miss" was also acceptable but please not "ma'am."

There were also those who would speak on top of others, even when not being addressed. So, for example, if I were asking Mrs. Smith what she would like to drink, Mr. Smith seated next to her would respond, "Gimme a Coke." Mr. Smith would only get that Coke *after* Mrs. Smith got her drink, and it would be given without a smile and without ice.

Complaining over meal choices was something else I didn't really understand. Why someone would get so bent out of shape over airline food was beyond me. There were times a passenger didn't get the chicken option, for instance, because we had already run out and then expected us to somehow find more. Other times a passenger who didn't receive a vegan choice believed he should be entitled to the crew food, like the fruit tray they might have spied in the galley. For the most part I would pack my own meals from home when going to work because the options on board usually weren't all that appetizing or healthy, for that matter. If passengers would only learn to either pre-order a meal or bring their own, the food drama would at least be alleviated. (Pre-orders still did not guarantee your meal, however, so if you had specific needs, play it safe and bring your own.)

To complicate matters further, the ill-mannered passengers could be further subcategorized into the entitled, sneaky, and sly. When one was a guest in someone's home, they should graciously accept what was being offered and given to them and not freely explore and grab anything deemed worthy. The aircraft was a flight attendant's home. Just like I did not appreciate when my children's friends would come over and open cupboards, helping themselves to food, I also did not appreciate passengers going into our galleys and helping themselves without asking. They believed to be entitled to any food, drink, magazine, newspaper, or anything else not bolted down. This sense of entitlement was not reserved solely for the galley area but also for our crew area. If we had crew seats available, we had to be careful when leaving items unattended, as they had a habit of disappearing into the hands of certain passengers. Even our own home-cooked meals were not safe when left alone. Trying to protect the little galley space we were given proved to be challenging at times when passengers exiting the lavatories would come and finish getting dressed there or do their yoga stretches or even pray. The galley was like our sanctuary where therapy sessions were held, all the juicy gossip was spilled, and laughs and tears were shared—protecting this area was critical.

Trying to get by me while I was working on a service trolley in the aisle was yet another popular peeve and boiled down to a lack of manners. Passengers would brush up against me, impatiently attempting to pass. Even when telling them to give me a minute so I could finish up with a passenger's drink order, they would still not back up far enough for me to be able to open a drawer. Elbows and knees would get hit, feet would get run over, and items would spill off the carts, yet passengers never even offered an apology. Except for the one guy who accidentally smacked me right on my butt as I was walking by. He was extremely embarrassed and apologized profusely.

The sneaky passengers couldn't be ignored either, especially when it came to pens. Simply put, if you were going to borrow a pen from a flight attendant, you had to eventually give it back. I shouldn't have had to go hunting down passengers and standing over them as they rifled through their personal belongings for *my* pen that they had now clearly stolen. If you did end up borrowing someone's pen, do not place it into your mouth or any other cavity for that matter. Many flight attendants I worked with refused to lend out any pens. Others, like myself, would only lend out the pens we had taken from our layover hotels. One colleague I knew bought a giant, two-foot pen she would lend if asked. Try stealing that one.

My favourites were the ones who thought they were being sly. They were the ones who would ask for a free kid's headset for their child because their kid didn't get one. *Oh really? I think grandma is wearing them.* Or, if that didn't work, they might pretend like the ones they got were broken. *Oh really? I'll throw the broken ones out for you and get you a new pair then.* Some would say they were friends with an employee in the company to get free items. *Oh really? Did your friend give you a free item voucher? No? Shucks, that's unfortunate.*

Some passengers believed if they did what they were told while you stood in front of them then they could do as they pleased as soon as you left. This was especially true when it pertained to turning off electronic devices. The moment I would walk away, that cell phone was back on again. This was like fighting a losing battle. It was pointless. Except for that one time a child was being disrespectful and not listening to me when I had already asked her twice to turn her gaming device off, since her parents apparently had no control. After I passed for the third time and found the device was back on again, I simply asked her for it. She was surprised but handed it to me anyway and her parents thanked me. My colleague and I enjoyed playing games on her device in the back galley.

Unruly parents and "blameless" parents were another peeve of mine. It always surprised me when parents would ask us to parent their children or speak on their behalf. Countless times parents had asked me to tell their child to put their seat belt on. *Ok, who's the parent here?* When I was a kid, a simple death glare or threat from my mother was all that was needed to make me behave.

This deserved a little back story. I grew up in a somewhat conservative Italian household. My parents were from the generation in which a little smack here and there was deemed necessary at times. Anything that was in reach to throw during a fight was considered fair game. I once watched my nonna (grandmother) throw a lemon straight across the room and hit my nonno (grandfather) on the side of the head one day while cooking. Apparently throwing lemons at someone in Ethiopia during Timkat (a celebration of the epiphany) meant they liked that person, but my grandparents were not Ethiopian, nor was it Timkat. They had gotten into an argument and then next thing you knew, we were dodging and ducking for cover.

If my father was out and my mother was left to deal with my defying behaviour, all she had to say was one line to put me into tears: *"Quando arriva il tuo papà, faremo i conti."* Translated literally this meant when your dad arrives, we will do math. As much as math could be scary, this line was not meant to be taken literally. What it really meant was when your dad arrives, you'd better run like the wind! It's basically equivalent to "wait 'til your father gets home."

I preferred threatening my own children more directly. Like the time they repeatedly rummaged through my storage bins after I had spent hours organizing them, and I told them the next time they touched them they'd get electrocuted. Yes, I was an evil mother, but my kids always put their seat belts on without a fuss. When I was little, I used to believe that if only I could run to the end of my driveway, I was home free. My dad couldn't punish me because I was somehow out of reach. It was just how I thought. Well, needless to say, I never did make it to the end of that driveway, and so it will forever remain a mystery.

Back to children on planes. If a child decided to run up and down the aisles with little regard for anyone else, and that child's parent decided to take a nap in their seat, that child might accidentally get run over by service trolleys. Just saying. (The tray tables by the way, were *not* to be used as seats for your tot.) While on the parent topic, I should address the diaper changing dilemma. No one wanted to see or smell a baby's dirty diaper, so please change diapers in the lavatories (as instructed by your flight attendant at the beginning of the flight) and not on the passenger seats. If you insisted on not listening and changing the diaper at your seat, passing the dirty diaper to a flight attendant to throw out was also a no-no. Other things not to pass to flight attendants to throw out included airsickness bags full of vomit, snot-filled tissues, chewed-up gum, half-eaten anything, retainers, and certainly not our pens! Garbage that you accumulated throughout the flight should, however, get collected, placed into a bag (if you did not have your own, you were welcome to use the airsickness bag), and thrown into the garbage trolley when it passed. A big thank you to all those who came prepared with their own disposable bag and antiseptic wipes.

You would be surprised to see just how disgusting the airplane would look once everyone had left. People were messy, and airplane passengers were no exception. There would be food remnants on the floor, chewed-up gum on the seat or tray table, dirty socks, dirty diapers, broken headsets, dandruff, and most disgustingly, skin flakes. Yes, skin flakes! This was more common than you'd think. Please moisturize if your skin was sunburned and was now peeling so you did not leave pieces of yourself behind.

Another thing I did not care to see were bare feet. I'd see them up on walls, on door slide bustles, on armrests, and even on tray tables. Watching people walk around barefoot was equally disgusting, especially when I'd see them entering the lavatories. For everyone's sake, please keep shoes on while on the plane or, at the very least, wear socks.

Although messy passengers were inevitable, passengers, for the most part, would thankfully board the plane, find their seats, and place larger items in the overhead bin and smaller items under the seat in front of them as instructed by the flight attendants and in an uneventful manner. Unfortunately, the annoyingly popular seat issues would soon come into play. Some passengers who had not pre-booked their seats and had arrived late for check-in would then get upset once they realized that they were not assigned seats next to their loved one. Unless this affected a small child, it was not on my priority list. I would still try my best to accommodate them, but these passengers would often lie as to when they checked in, which was completely unnecessary. The boarding card would soon reveal the truth anyway. For example, if your boarding card said you were passenger number 331 and there were 332 passenger seats on that aircraft, it wasn't going to look favourable on you.

If you were lucky enough to not be on a full aircraft, it was rude to try to keep three seats all to yourself while others were squished. I had passengers purposely seat themselves in a centre seat to try to deter others from sitting next to them so that they could then lie down. If I had a big, tall single guy sitting next to a mom and her baby, where do you think I would try to move him to? That's right. Big guy coming through. Then there were those who would help themselves to just any random seat before we had even finished boarding. I had a passenger move at least three times once because he refused to take his own assigned seat.

"Is it going to be a full flight?" a passenger asked me as he was passing me in the aisle during boarding.

"Yes, it is." I responded.

"Oh, I was hoping to get a window seat," he said, showing me his boarding card so I could see where he was seated.

He was assigned a middle seat towards the back. I knew he probably wasn't going to have any luck, as no one ever wanted the middle seat, but I tried to assure him anyway. "Once boarding is finished, I'll see what I can do."

I assumed he would go sit in his seat for the time being, but instead, I saw him place himself at a window seat in the emergency row (SMH). Sure enough, the passenger who had reserved that seat arrived shortly after, and my seat stealer had to move. But he didn't move to his assigned seat—he chose yet another window seat, this time a little farther back. I didn't want him to keep inconveniencing others, so I started walking towards him. Before I could get to him (the aisles were still crowded with boarding passengers), I could see he was once again being made to move. He now slipped himself into the window seat directly behind the one he was in. *You've got to be kidding me*, I thought, now on a mission to bolt this guy down to his middle seat. I managed to maneuver my way down the aisle to where my stubborn passenger was.

"Sir, you're going to need to take your own seat. I told you I'd help once boarding was finished."

"But no one's in this seat," he responded.

"For now," I told him. "Like I said we are a full flight today, I'm sure someone's coming."

"Excuse me, I believe he's in my seat," I heard a passenger say from behind me.

"And here she is," I told my window-seat-stealing passenger.

He tried to ask her if she would switch seats with him, but when she heard it was a middle seat, it was a definite no. All the window seats were now occupied, and I was over trying to help him, so seat stealer sat in his middle seat for the duration of the flight.

Seat grievances were not limited to location, unfortunately. Passengers would inevitably find something to complain about even when seated in their pre-booked seat. Like the ever-popular issue of seat reclining. Once in your seat, the rule was to wait until the seat-belt sign has been turned off before reclining. And yes, the person in front of you was allowed to recline theirs as well. It was one inch of comfort, so let's not be petty over this. Although this rule was enforced during meal service, it was only polite to bring the seat back upright during this time. What I could never understand was why some passengers believed it was okay to recline their *own* seats while attempting to block the passengers in front from reclining theirs. I felt like I was talking to my teenage children when I'd be called over to deal with a reclining-seat issue between two passengers.

The tight quarters resulted in seating drama as well. Just so everyone was aware, the unwritten rule when it came to armrests was that if you were unfortunate enough to be seated in a middle seat, the armrests were respectfully yours to use. My family had a hard time accepting this rule when I was stuck with the centre seat on a ten-hour flight en route to Africa. They not only broke the armrest rule but also the one-cushion rule when they ended up using my armrests and spilling over onto my already uncomfortable seat.

In my household, we had an additional rule when it came to seating. It was the one-cushion-per-person rule when sitting together on the couch. Sometimes we needed to remind our kids to stay on their own cushion. It was like shouting out "shotgun" to secure the front seat or calling dibs on something—a simple but effective rule in peace keeping. If only things were as simple as that on board. I could just imagine passengers coming on board complaining that their seat was taken, to which I would simply reply, "Well, they called dibs."

If passengers weren't complaining about seat grievances, then they'd move on to baggage storage. Some passengers absolutely refused to part from their bags, even if they were merely being placed in the storage bin directly above their heads. Others, on the other hand, would try to take up an entire compartment solely for their own personal belongings and would become annoyed when there were other items in there, such as our emergency equipment. Once I was assisting with boarding when an elderly passenger became extremely disgruntled because the overhead bin directly above him was already occupied with emergency equipment. He wanted me to move it elsewhere, but when I explained why this was not feasible, he grew even angrier. The fact that there was room for his bags in all the other adjacent bins did not matter to him. Then he looked towards the front and saw that the passengers in club class were being offered orange juice.

"Why don't *I* get offered orange juice?" he snarked.

Instead of responding with "because you're in economy," I decided to bite my tongue and politely asked, "Would you care for some orange juice?"

When I returned from the back galley with an orange juice for both him and his wife, I knew his wife must have scolded him while I was gone because his demeanor had completely changed in a matter of minutes. As I passed them their drinks, he apologized for his behaviour. If only all *loco* passengers had a kick-ass wife who could beat some sense into them.

The overhead compartments were *shared* compartments. If there was already something there, you should *not* attempt to remove it. If the bin closest to you could not accommodate your bag, use another one. You'd think placing bags in bins was a no-brainer, but you'd be surprised. Remember those wooden blocks we were given in kindergarten that we'd have to match up to its corresponding shape on a container in order to fit it through? Sometimes, as I would watch passengers trying to fit their bag into a bin, I couldn't help but think back to this and wonder if they were deprived from playing with these wooden blocks as children.

Then there were those passengers who did not even attempt to stow their bag at all. In fact, I had a "princess passenger" once who came on, found her seat, placed her carry-on suitcase in the aisle, and buckled herself in. Being the passive-aggressive person I was, I walked up the aisle, stepped *over* her suitcase, and proceeded to point out all the bin space we had. Unless you were short, elderly, or physically impaired, my back would not be subjected to excessive and unnecessary physical demands. Even though there were supposed to be restrictions in place as to the size and weight of carry-on items, somehow those one-hundred-pound hockey-sized duffle bags still seemed to make their appearance on board.

Sometimes when the flight was completely full and the passengers had carried on more than their share, we had to off-load excess bags, which would then be placed into the checked baggage hold. If this occurred, always remember not to check anything personal you didn't need, such as a passport, a wallet, medication, or a prosthetic limb. Over time, there wasn't much that could faze a flight attendant. I had a passenger once who asked me where he could put his spare leg. Another asked where she could place her mother. (She had meant the urn with her mother's ashes.) Once all the baggage issues had been resolved and those bins finally did get closed, passengers should refrain from reopening them unless they were going to close them again. I was constantly closing bins when walking through the aisles, wondering why passengers just couldn't do this simple task. But then I would brush it off as I thought of my own husband who still could not seem to turn off lights or close cupboard doors.

It was those simple tasks that seemed most impossible for some passengers, and seat-belt unbuckling was no exception. As much as passengers believed it to be true, touchdown did not mean the immediate unbuckling of seat belts, the opening of bins, and the turning on of cell phones. Inevitably though this was always the case. As soon as the tires hit the tarmac, I could hear the seat belts unbuckling and the *ding, ding, ding* of all the cell phones coming to life. Those who would also immediately stand to open the bins and get their luggage were the most frustrating because now they were risking hurting others just so they could have their bags in hand first. I couldn't understand this because they still had to wait for those seated in front of them to disembark anyway. These were the times I would secretly wish the captain would slam on the brakes just enough to make those passengers faceplant in the aisle.

The last few peeves I'll be mentioning—albeit minor—were nonetheless annoying and thus worth mentioning. It was usually many of those seemingly "little things" that added up over time, so please excuse the rant. There were those who we called button abusers. If you needed something from the flight attendant, passengers should feel free to press that call button—*once*. If your neighbour just called a flight attendant over, you could also ask for something instead of waiting until he or she has left and then immediately pressing the call button. Do not bang on the television screen in the seatbacks as this could disturb the passenger in front. Equally disturbing to a passenger seated in front was a child kicking their seat. And only involve a flight attendant in these petty issues once attempting to speak to your neighbour about them yourself.

Not everyone wanted to hear your movie or music, so please keep your volume under control. If you placed your meal tray or trash on the floor, you shouldn't expect the flight attendant to get it. If the crew member's language skills in your mother tongue were not "proper" enough for you, do not roll your eyes but rather just appreciate the fact that at least they tried. If you pre-ordered a special meal (vegetarian, kosher, etc.), do not request something else, and if you didn't pre-order a meal, don't ask for one. Also, don't ask silly questions you already knew the answer to, such as asking if you can open the emergency door in flight, have a quick smoke, or drink your own alcohol. *No, no, and no. Duh.* If you'd like to know what we flew over, don't wait an hour later to ask. Do not argue when a flight attendant has told you that a debit card was *not*, in fact, a credit card and therefore could not be used for in-flight purchases. Do not sit in the emergency exit window seats if you were going to ignore the flight attendant or pretend to sleep when being briefed. Do not sit on the slide bustle right on top of the sticker that showed to not sit on the slide bustle. Lastly, do not attempt to use the lavatories when the seat belt sign was on, especially just before landing. I always made sure to check the lavatories in my section before buckling into my jump seat before landing, but on one occasion after I had already sat down, a passenger snuck into the lavatory from behind me without my notice. It was only after we had touched down and he exited the lav during the taxiing did I know he had landed in there.

Something else that was pointless was telling passengers on my Dutch flights that I was not, in fact, Dutch and could not understand them. They insisted on speaking Dutch to me anyway, so instead of arguing I would simply smile and nod. Funny enough the contrary would happen on my Italian flights. No one believed I could speak Italian, so when they would hear me speaking in their language, they'd first look extremely surprised, and then they'd want to be best friends. The elderly men were the friendliest. One of them offered me a marriage proposal, another wanted me to visit him at his place in Rome, another gave me a silver charm pendant, which I think I still have, and another serenaded me in the galley. Apparently, these were the men I seemed to attract.

End rant.

Even though the peeves associated with flying were many, there were equally as many pleasures. Thankfully, many of my passengers were well-mannered and courteous. But this chapter was about the peeves, so for now I'll just say thank you—it was a pleasure.

The Laughs

Flight attendants would try to keep things light and entertaining while on the job because being confined in a tin can at 38,000 feet for hours on end with the same people could eventually lead to boredom if your flight was lacking in crazies. Normally if I were bored at home I could always go for a walk with the dog, chat with my friends, or turn to the internet for some quick entertainment. None of those options were available while I was at work, however. We remained disconnected from the rest of the world, except of course when there was a major sports game on, and the captain would check in with ground control for updates, thereby keeping our tin can in the loop. By playing friendly, competitive games with bets, having a not-taking-things-seriously attitude, trying to make each other laugh both on and off the plane, and being good sports about the unintentional laughs, flight crew remained, for the most part, entertained.

As a means of breaking the monotony of our routine while on duty, the crew would sometimes compete or play games together. The cup-stacking competition was both fun and productive. After finishing a beverage service, we would collect all the used cups, and because we were always so short on garbage space, we would stack the cups into one another to make more room before placing them into the garbage trolley. The trick was in who could stack the tallest pile of cups before having to throw them into the bin. This had to be performed one-handed, as the other hand was used to collect the cups from the passengers and push the garbage trolley along. I'm not sure who held the record in this, since flight attendants were all a bunch of liars and cheaters, or maybe I was confusing them with my family. When it came to playing Monopoly with my family, for instance, the winner was always determined by the best cheater. (We really needed the cheater's edition of any game.)

If we were on a two-aisle aircraft, competition usually existed between the left and the right sides. There would be smack talk on which side had the better passengers, got the better service, and so on. At the beginning of every flight, positions were assigned and depending on what your position was for the day, you'd either be working the left or the ride side of the plane. Sometimes the flight attendants would egg the passengers on to boast their side even further. The duty-free boutique displays on the trolleys became storefront worthy in the attempt to sell more products on one side versus the other. Which side had the faster meal and beverage service, the cleaner lavatories, the tidier cabin—nothing was off the table. This friendly competition was all it would take to lighten the mood at times and keep things entertaining.

Galley games would consist of Hedbanz, charades, Pictionary, crosswords, and trivia, just to name a few. We had to be careful not to get too excited when playing these games, though, since our galley curtains were not as soundproof as many passengers hoped. On one particular flight, I was working in the back galley with two soccer-loving flight attendants, who thought it would be fun to have a little scrimmage using a scrunched-up ball of paper. They were trying to score by kicking the "ball" against the wall behind one another while we "spectators" egged them on. The game lasted no longer than five minutes because apparently two grown men couldn't keep the noise level down when competing over a paper ball.

Betting was extremely popular among the crew as well. This did not involve cash but rather just sheer satisfaction and bragging rights. We'd bet on just about anything from ETA*; length of turbulence; length of delay; which oven would become inoperative in flight; and who among our passengers would be the complainer, the overbearing and annoyingly friendly talkative one, the drinker, or the infamous stander who would keep getting in our way for the entire duration of the flight. Betting really helped keep the in-flight atmosphere light and friendly.

What I learned from being a flight attendant for so many years was how to not take things too seriously. This was yet another tactic to lighten the mood and beat any boredom during a flight. Travelling stressed a lot of people out, and we tended to be the ones they lashed out on. Once we took off, we were pretty much trapped. I used to witness new flight attendants who would take things personally and end up leaving upset, but eventually they, too, learned how to brush things off. I once witnessed a flight director who was dealing with an irate passenger who threatened to never fly with our company again. The flight director responded by saying, "Do you promise?" The expression on the passenger's face was priceless. She was so taken aback by his question that she didn't know what to say after that and simply returned to her seat.

Not taking things too seriously didn't mean not performing my job properly. In fact, I took pride in providing my passengers with exceptional customer service, but I also participated in the behind-the-scenes antics and shenanigans. Much like being the new kid in high school, there was a rite of passage the newbies were expected to endure. On one occasion, one of the senior flight attendants I was working with thought it would be a good idea to tell the newbie that it was the most junior's job to go into the cargo hold of the plane and feed the dogs. Not knowing how to do this, she was told she needed to go in through the cockpit floor and once down in the belly, she would find the dog food. The newbies were always eager to impress and too naive to question a senior flight attendant, so she proceeded to enter the cockpit. That was as far as she made it before being questioned by the pilots.

Sometimes merely changing up our uniform pieces was all that was needed to lighten the mood. Neck scarves would be used as babushkas, hair wraps, or even made into flower-shaped chokers. (I still have the how-to video made by a colleague.) One girl I knew used to bring along realistic-looking, fake gag teeth. They were the most ugly, rotten, yellow-stained teeth I had ever seen, and she wore them with the utmost pride while happily performing her passenger services in the aisles and smiling away. If we had had an award for best actress in flight, she would have won it hands down. *Bravo!* The passengers would try to act normal when they'd notice her teeth, so as not to offend her when she'd speak to them, but their initial surprised reaction could not be hidden, and the crew would burst out laughing.

Keeping in theme with lightening the in-flight mood, the crew enjoyed trying to make each other laugh, especially when it was highly inappropriate. The commonality among many flight attendants was our twisted humour. During the safety demonstration (demo) shown before every take off, we were supposed to stand by our jump seats and face the passengers to ensure they were paying attention (or at least being silent so others could). The flight attendants whose jump seats were behind the passengers, and thus didn't have to participate, took full advantage of this opportunity. This was their chance to do anything in their power to break the others into laughter. This was like how anyone who visited London, England, found it necessary to provoke reaction from the Queen's Guard.

Sometimes technical difficulties would occur, and we would have to resort to conducting a manual safety demo instead of using the video. One of those times was on my route to Frankfurt. Normally we would conduct the safety demo only in English and French, our two official languages. On this day, however, our flight director thought it would be a good idea to also do it in German, since most of our passengers were of German descent, and she herself could speak the language. Who was I to question this? I was a junior flight attendant at the time, and she was my superior.

No one thought much of it until the crew and I were standing in the middle of the aisles at our designated locations not understanding a word the flight director was speaking over the intercom. It started off okay as the flight director began the manual safety demonstration in English. "Carefully review the safety card in the seat pocket in front of you," she announced. I held up the card, demonstrated its location, and opened it up for all to see. Next was the demonstration of the emergency exits, the floor-level lighting, the usage of the seat belt, the oxygen mask, and finally the life jacket. Easy peasy, lemon squeezy, until the flight director started repeating the entire demonstration in German. I obviously knew what order everything was to be shown but had no idea at what point in the demonstration she was at, nor did any of my other colleagues. I tried to keep roughly the same pace as I would when demonstrating in English, but my actions and what was being said were obviously not in sync, as the passengers who were watching me began laughing. I likely looked like one of those old, poorly dubbed films in which the spoken words didn't match the characters' moving mouths. Those who weren't paying attention earlier (as many didn't) were suddenly keen to learn what to do in case of an emergency. It didn't help that our only German-speaking crew member was making the announcements from behind a wall and didn't witness our failing act. She kept on talking, so we kept on demonstrating. It wasn't until the amount of laughter coming from the cabin became so loud that she realized what was happening. The passengers closest to me were trying to be kind and helpful by telling me what I should be displaying, but with the high level of laughter and outright disaster happening, I might as well have been waving a white flag. I eventually joined the rest of the cabin and started crying in laughter. Embarrassed was an understatement. As my mother always said, *"meglio ridere che piangere,"* which meant better to laugh than to cry; although I was doing both at the time. My colleagues and I finished the demonstration well ahead of the announcements and just stood there laughing and waiting for the flight director to finish talking. In retrospect, she figured she should have read

English, immediately followed by German after each item was being demonstrated, which was already common practice with our usual English/French or French/English safety demos. *You think?*

Some of the best laughs were those completely unintentional. Being a bilingual company meant accents could alter certain words. My favourite was the time my French-speaking flight director made a P.A. announcement to share which movie would be shown on the flight (before individual passenger screens became a thing). "On today's flight we will have the pleasure of presenting *Shrek da turd*," she announced. (*Shrek the Third.*) She didn't realize why everyone was laughing until someone pointed it out to her.

Words like *da wedder* (*the weather*) and *dare* (*there*) were also commonly heard words but obviously not as funny. My Newfoundlander father-in-law (a.k.a. fodder), like the French, liked to drop *t*'s for *d*'s in words. Since he liked to refer to me as a mudder (mother), and I enjoyed teasing him, I thought it would be funny after completing the Tough Mudder obstacle race one year to purchase a mug for myself to show him that I was one tough mudder. If you can't beat 'em . . .

Travelling internationally meant being exposed to not only varying accents but also unfamiliar words or terminology that were common in a particular country. Deciphering these "foreign" words helped keep things light and interesting and usually gave us a laugh. I thought after twenty plus years I had finally been able to decipher the Scottish accent until an elderly lady had stopped me in the aisle and spoke to me for a solid two minutes.

"My sister and I are headed to . . . ," she started, but this was where it got fuzzy.

"I'm sorry, what?" I finally asked her when she was clearly done talking and waiting for me to respond. I was hoping I would have picked up enough words to make sense of the conversation and at least give her a half-decent answer, but there was no fooling her; she had lost me after the first seven words. She laughed it off and continued speaking with another Scottish passenger instead.

I found out that *plaster* meant an adhesive bandage when a little English girl kept asking me for it. I thought she was asking for plasticine, until she eventually showed me the cut on her finger. Every time I was saying no when asked if we had lemonade, I hadn't realized I was lying, until a passenger pointed out that their neighbour was given one by another flight attendant. The British version of lemonade was 7UP with a lemon wedge, in case you didn't know. Another time I thought a passenger was asking for Susie, so since I didn't know anyone named Susie at my company, I asked another crew member if she knew who Susie was. As it turned out, my Asian passenger was looking for sushi.

The laughs and shenanigans did not necessarily end just because we had stepped off the aircraft either. When leaving from a hotel on a layover, we had to be on the crew shuttle bus by a certain time, or else you had to fend for yourself and find transportation to the airport at your own expense. I was in London on one of these occasions, when the entire crew less one was on the bus and ready to go. We still had a few minutes left before departure, but because this crew all shared the same evil humour and knew each other quite well, we thought we'd prank our missing colleague into thinking she was late and that we were leaving without her. We asked the driver if he would do us the favour of pretending to drive away when he saw her exiting the hotel, and being the gracious driver he was, he obliged. It wondered marvelously. She panicked when she saw us starting to leave without her and ran after the bus with luggage in tow, yelling for us to wait. We looped around the circular driveway while she frantically followed in hot pursuit, only to return exactly where we had started. My now out-of-breath colleague hopped onto a bus filled with laughter. Just as we had thought, she was a good sport about it and laughed it off with us. We blamed the bus driver.

The phrase, "all for one and one for all," did not always apply to flight attendants on layovers. I was walking around the streets of Venice with a couple of colleagues when one of them made the mistake of eyeing a handbag for a little too long. It was common to see illegal street vendors selling cheap knock-off designer name handbags, wallets, or sunglasses off blankets on the streets. The sellers were very persistent, particularly if you seemed to take any interest in their products. If you didn't want to be harassed, you would ignore looking at what they were selling and keep walking. When my colleague eyed their handbag, it was game on for the seller. He immediately picked up the bag and insisted she buy it. My other colleague and I continued walking. This was her mistake and she had to take responsibility. How else was she going to learn? She kept trying to say no to the seller and then just started walking away towards us.

The street vendor followed her for a couple of minutes before finally giving up. Having now ditched the seller, she looked at me and my friend who were still laughing uncontrollably and thanked us for having her back. I'm sure she never made that mistake again, however.

In Glasgow, I made the mistake of trusting my jokester friend. We were on the train with our daughters, returning from Edinburgh, when I asked my colleague if she wouldn't mind taking my picture with my daughter. We had been airdropping pictures to each other all day so she simply used her phone and said she would just send it to me. What I didn't know was that she was going to take a close up of just me and airdrop it to a stranger on the train. An older woman turned to look at me quizzically from across the aisle while also looking at her phone and my friend started cracking up with laughter. Well played my friend, well played.

Whoever said laughter was the best medicine could not have been more right. Not only could the job of a flight attendant be stressful, but it could also be boring during those long overnight stretches when most passengers were sleeping and you could not. Playing games, engaging in in-flight shenanigans, poking fun of one another, and even placing non-monetary bets were all part of the fun. Sporting a fun attitude even seemed to make the time pass quicker. It was our form of entertainment when disconnected from the rest of the world, and I would always be grateful for it.

*ETA: This refers to the estimated time of arrival.

*popping a slide: Not as in baseball when sliding into a base, but rather this refers to the unintentional deployment of an inflatable emergency slide when opening an aircraft's door in emergency mode. This was a huge no-no.

Chapter Nine

The Crew Drama

Drama was always entertaining, especially if you weren't the one involved; however, as much fun as it was to watch, it was still better to watch it in the movies rather than to see it on the plane. Who was I kidding? Everyone had a cell phone now, and capturing the right drama at the right time could make all the difference in your video going viral! It also made for juicy gossip stories once home. As much as flight attendants enjoyed talking about passenger drama, ironically crew drama tended to be juicier. Crew drama was often in the form of arguments, disagreements, and confrontations. Whether it was due to stress, miscommunication, personality conflicts, power struggles, entitlement, or changes in protocol, when the drama monster was released, it usually became an award-winning show.

Some crew members lacked both professionalism and tactfulness when dealing with issues or arguments, which made for some interesting, but also sometimes awkward, entertainment. I wasn't sure what had happened prior to hearing two of my colleagues yelling at each other in Greek from across the aisles, but it had attracted a lot of attention. Since flight attendants tended to be multilingual, sometimes they would speak in a different language from most of the passengers to be discreet. However, there was nothing discreet about this instance when it became a full-on yelling match. Whether people understood what was being said or not did not matter at this point. They were being inconsiderate of everyone around them. Although by the looks on the passengers' faces, they hadn't really minded. I was embarrassed for their actions, nonetheless, because it diminished the professionalism of our company. And maybe it boiled down to a personality conflict; however, I felt like a mother apologizing on behalf of her possessed child, who was having a meltdown in the middle of a mall. (True story: I was once *that* mother, and my eldest daughter was *that* child.)

Whenever I had a quarrel with a fellow crew member, I would attempt to address it head-on, trying not to involve anyone else. When the captain of one particular flight took offence to having to wait for his personal duty-free order at the beginning of a seven-hour flight, instead of talking to me directly about it, he spoke to the flight director who then informed me about his annoyance. Apparently because I told him we were busy now and I would deliver his bottle of whatever-it-was from duty-free later, it angered him. *How dare I not drop everything I was doing to attend to his needs immediately?* (Had I mentioned the god complex some pilots possessed?) When interacting with the flight director after this trivial incident, he would repeatedly say, "Sorry I'm busy," as a jab towards me. At any rate, I let him stew in his anger for the duration of the flight while I tended to the passengers' needs, and when I found some time (towards the end of the flight), I brought him his duty-free order.

"I'm so happy I was able to provide you with some entertainment for the flight," I told him as he looked over his shoulder at me when I entered the cockpit with his order.

He had nothing to say in response and simply turned back at the controls in front of him, with not even a thanks. "If you had something to say, you could have said it to me," I continued, talking to the back of his head now. Crickets.

The first officer gave me one of those sympathetic shoulder shrugs, as if to say, "What can you do?"

"You're welcome," I said sarcastically while placing the duty-free on the floor and then walked out. I only saw the pilot one other time after this, and when he noticed it was me, he avoided making eye contact.

Another time, a confrontation between a different captain and a cabin crew member was not so discreet. During turbulence, the pilots would switch on the seat-belt sign if they deemed it necessary for everyone's safety. On this day, we were operating a turn to Punta Cana and had just started our BOB and beverage service when the sign-belt sign was illuminated. We therefore had to stop our services, and while the flight director made his "please fasten your seat belts" announcement, we secured our trolleys back into the galley, checked the cabin to ensure everyone was wearing their seatbelts, and then secured ourselves into our jump seats. Before some of us had even the chance to buckle up, the seat-belt sign was turned back off, and we were able to continue with the services.

Within a few minutes of restarting, the seat-belt sign was illuminated *yet* again, and the entire process was repeated. Now back for the third time, we carried on and managed to complete most of our sections before that seat-belt sign was once again turned on. As annoying as it could get, I didn't give it much thought because sometimes we just had bumpy flights, and it couldn't be avoided. The other flight attendants looked just as annoyed as I was, but flights with sporadic turbulence were not uncommon, so we knew it was simply bad timing for us, and we had to comply with safety measures. Sometimes being inconvenienced by the weather was part of our job. I had flights in which we hadn't been able to finish services or even get around to starting some of them due to turbulence. We simply had to deal with it as best as we could.

The flight director was not impressed with the captain's use of the seat-belt sign, however, and was not exactly diplomatic when voicing his opinions. When we landed back at home base, we had a debriefing* before being allowed to leave.

"You made us look like a bunch of buffoons," the flight director said to the captain without wasting any time and getting right to the point. He thought we looked ridiculous coming and going with the trolleys in the aisles.

The captain retaliated, as his authority was now being questioned over the use of the seat-belt sign. "Did you think I was doing it for fun?" he asked not expecting a response. "When it comes to turbulence, I would never risk jeopardizing our safety. If I have to turn on the seat-belt sign, I will. Even if it means you guys will have to stop and restart your services."

"If you're going to turn it on, then keep it on for longer than two minutes so we don't look like idiots," the flight director said.

The pilot did not concede. "Don't tell me how to do my job. I know what I'm doing."

At this point I stopped paying attention to the arguing because neither were willing to back down, and it had become increasingly awkward for the rest of us who were not even involved. I just wanted to go home. We were eventually dismissed, and a week later none other than the same captain was in my annual training class. "So how about that flight director?" he asked me, referring to our mutual flight. I smiled and looked away. He got the hint.

Sometimes passengers would feel entitled because they worked at the airport. They expected free items or believed the rules didn't apply to them, which could end in drama when they didn't get their way. If an airport employee presented a voucher (which many would receive with their ticket), then they would be given their choice of complimentary item. Easy. If everyone had checked in and there was still space available in club class, then it would be offered to the most senior colleague or their companion. Unless an economy passenger wanted to upgrade at the last minute, then they had priority obviously. Also, easy. And, if we asked the passengers to do something, it was assumed for *all* passengers. This request should have been super easy.

As easy as things should have been, I still had an air traffic controller who had a temper tantrum on board. I was walking down the aisle offering food items from our bistro menu when he stopped me to request a turkey sandwich.

"Sure," I said, "here you are." I passed him the sandwich. "That'll be $8.99," I told him.

He slowly grabbed the sandwich while looking at me in an odd fashion. "But I work at the airport," he told me, thinking maybe I forgot.

"Yes, I know," I assured him. "But unless you have a flight coupon, it's still $8.99."

He reluctantly stood up to reach into the overhead bin. "My wallet is in my bag."

He was probably hoping I'd tell him not to worry about it, but instead I said, "No problem, I can wait."

He brought his bag down but then seemed to have a change of thought. "Aren't I supposed to get it for free? They didn't charge me anything on the way out."

Great, once again someone wasn't following the rules, and now, I was the bad guy. "Yeah, they should have charged you. It doesn't work that way. You're not entitled to freebies because you work at the airport."

"Can you just get the flight director?" he asked me, obviously not believing what I said.

"Sure."

I left the trolley with my partner so she could continue with the service while I went to talk to my flight director, knowing perfectly well that he would still have to pay for his sandwich because she had already confirmed earlier on at the beginning of the flight that our air traffic controller was to be given no freebies unless he had coupons. She followed me down the aisle to his seat and basically reiterated what I had already told him. Not impressed, he tossed me back the turkey sandwich and commenced his sulking. *Wow,* I thought, *what a child.*

When we were preparing to land, I asked this same still-sulking man-child to raise his seat back, and instead of simply complying, he thrust his seat back and forth.

"It's already up!" he yelled, causing the other passengers to take notice and shake their heads in disbelief.

"Actually, it's not," I told him. He angrily pressed the button on his armrest, and the seat back raised a couple of inches. "Now it's up," I said and walked away.

On one layover flight, when I brought my husband with me, he had stayed behind at check-in to wait and see if he'd be able to get assigned the last club class seat available. The rule was he had to wait until check-in closed in case others wished to purchase a seat at the last minute or in case other employees of higher seniority were entitled to the seat first. His patience paid off and he was assigned the seat. While we were boarding, I discovered another employee was travelling with her spouse and was now attempting to have my husband bumped out of club class for her husband to have that seat. I didn't know who she was and so figured she was probably one of the newer hires I hadn't worked with yet. First, she hadn't followed the rules of having him wait at the check-in counter. Had she done this, she would have known that I had greater seniority than her, and her husband wouldn't have gotten the seat. Second, she assumed the ground agent would take care of things once on board, and so she ended up inconveniencing not only this agent but also my husband and me because now he had to figure out who was entitled to the club seat. Since my husband didn't know what my seniority or employee number was, the ground agent now had to barrel his way past all the passengers who were in the middle of the aisles to get to the rear of the aircraft and verify my company ID. My husband enjoyed his club seat.

You know how people say when you're in a certain profession that you are the worst at following your own rules or taking your own advice? For example, the landscaper who has the ugliest lawn, the policeman who likes to speed when off duty, or the chef who makes mac and cheese at home. Flight attendants make some of the worst passengers. When they'd be deadheading or travelling on vacation, many times I found myself having to tell them to put their seat belts on, store their bags, or turn off their phones. During turbulence they'd be trying to use the lavatories or grab something from the overhead bins. It was frustrating when I'd see crew members do exactly what we didn't want passengers doing.

On one particular flight, the seat-belt signs were on, and we were getting ready to take off when one of my deadheaders thought it would be a good time to change his outfit. He opened a bin (all bins had already been closed by this time), removed his bag, placed it on our crew seats, and started rummaging through it to grab his lighter clothes. I reminded him that we were leaving soon, even though I knew that he knew, and he should be sitting like everyone else. He said he would be quick and proceeded to the lavatory to get changed. I looked at my colleague and we both rolled our eyes. He exited the lavatory now changed, threw his luggage back into the bin, and returned to his seat. I now quickly did a seat-belt check, and of course had to remind him to buckle up. During the flight he kept entering the galley and helping himself to whatever he chose. He made himself a coffee, grabbed a snack, a drink, and so on. When passengers waiting to use the lavatory would see him grabbing items in the galley and give me strange looks, I'd have to explain that he was a flight attendant.

It was especially annoying when those same crew members made it a point to let *all* the other passengers around them know they were flight attendants. I didn't understand this because this didn't mean they were exempt from following the rules, and so it only resulted in making some passengers feel inferior. When I travelled as a passenger, I made a concerted effort to *not* draw any attention to myself. Unlike my son the time we were travelling together, and his headset volume was obviously too loud as he yelled out to his sister, "Put it on channel 1!" for everyone to hear.

The worst drama I had ever witnessed between a flight attendant and a passenger was when a passenger took a flight attendant's picture. I wasn't sure why the picture was taken or what words were exchanged before this happened, but that flight attendant snatched the disposable camera out of his hands, stomped on it, and threw it into the garbage trolley. (This was before everyone owned a cell phone.) One thing for sure was that this didn't exactly happen because my colleague was being camera shy. I didn't know what the outcome from this was, but I did know that I ended up having to pick up the slack for the remainder of the flight, since my partner was now out of order.

Sometimes the crew drama was a result of something as simple as which way we would do the on-board services, even though there would already be a standard that we were supposed to follow. They varied according to various factors, such as aircraft type, domestic or international route, length of flight, and time of departure. The "service flows" did not always suit all flights because many times things did not go as planned, so if there was a delay, for example, passengers might now be hungry and want to eat first versus getting a drink. Or maybe the passengers were boarding an aircraft that had been sitting on the tarmac with no air conditioning, and they required water before even taking off. I was all for being flexible and doing whatever meant the passengers were happy and comfortable, but others were very much by the book, no matter what. Deviating from the standard meant more paperwork for the flight director because he or she would have to explain why this was done, and sometimes they just couldn't be bothered. Other times it would be the flight director who would want to initiate the change, and there would be pushback from a flight attendant who didn't agree.

On the morning of one of my turns to the Caribbean, we had a departure delay due to the cargo door being unable to close. All the passengers were already on board, and we were now stuck waiting for a mechanic to fix the door so that we could leave. Because we knew it was going to be a while, the flight director told us we would do a ground service. While on the ground, the trolleys were not allowed in the aisles, so any services we did had to be done by hand. Normally this meant simply handing out water, but, on this day, the flight director wanted us to serve coffee and tea because she figured it was early and the passengers would appreciate it. I knew this wasn't going to go well. The senior crew I was working with in the back galley seemed to also agree. The flight director insisted, and we proceeded serving hot beverages using a tray. It was not only painstakingly slow but also dangerous and impractical for those who didn't drink coffee or tea (such as the many small children). After a few minutes of following orders, one of the senior flight attendants in charge of the back galley had had enough and told the flight director we were no longer going to serve any more passengers. The two argued back and forth while the rest of us started putting things away. The majority ruled, and I didn't mind in the least. (In hindsight, this drama was a little tame. Well, if anything you learned about service flows.)

As much as the drama made for good conversation once at home, I still would have preferred if everyone checked their emotional baggage but didn't forget to carry-on their manners and common sense. (My slice of cheese for this chapter.) Being confined to one space for long periods of time did not always bring out the best in people, including crew. As much as I was grateful to be able to visit so many amazing cities all over the world while at the same time getting paid, the challenge was sometimes in the journey there. For flight attendants the WWJD (What would Jesus do?) way of thinking could be replaced with WINTCMUR (Will I need to call my union rep?).

. . .

*debriefing: Not as in the removal of underwear but rather this is a meeting between all the crew members after a flight.

Chapter Ten

The Embarrassments

As much as flight attendants tried to display a professional appearance while at work, they still experienced unpredictable, embarrassing moments. It would have been no big deal if I could have simply chuckled along with the passengers, except that these moments were also happening to me—on vacations, in my everyday life, at the airport, while in flight, and even on layovers. When my children would tell me that I was embarrassing, they weren't kidding. I seemed to have a knack for attracting humiliation at my own expense. As much as I enjoyed laughing, I found others enjoyed laughing just as much, particularly at me and especially my own loving family.

Unfortunately for me, my shadow of embarrassment liked to follow me everywhere I went, even on vacations. My family and I went on a little four-day adventure to New York City, and, being the expert traveller I believed I now was thanks to my flying career, I figured going through airport security would be a breeze. I knew exactly what would be required of us and made sure to pack accordingly. One by one my family walked through the metal detector, and their carry-ons went through the X-ray machine without a hitch, and then it was my turn. "Ma'am, I'm going to need you to open your bag." The security officer rummaged through my carry-on until he found a pair of Crayola scissors—my blunt, rounded crafting scissors, which one of my kids had most likely planted in there. The same kids who, along with their father, had now ditched me at the security hall while the scissors were getting confiscated and I was getting a lecture. (My next book should be titled *When a Nerd Marries a Punk and Has Asshole Children*.)

View from Markwe Cave—if not scared to look

During a grander vacation in Zimbabwe, my family and I had visited the Markwe Caves to see the bushman paintings. We had to climb the side of a steep and rocky hill to arrive at the entrance of this cave site. I didn't think much of it as I carefully watched my footing and followed our two guides. My eldest daughter thought it was too steep and chose not to climb the final stretch into the cave. I should have done the same. Once at the top, I turned around to take a picture, and that's when I freaked out.

Me holding on for dear life behind the guide while my daughter Sarah is trying to hide her annoyance

All I could think was, *I'm going to slide off this edge and die.* I crouched as far back into the cave as I possibly could and gripped hold of a rock barrier. When one of the guides noticed me crying, he came and stood in front of me, trying to reassure me while the other guide continued with the explanation of the cave and its paintings. It had something to do with chiefs and royalty. I didn't really know. I was crying and thinking of my death at the time. My husband was supportive and came to my aid, but I could tell my kids were trying hard to contain their laughter. The guides were extremely patient with me as they led me back. Shaking all the way, I slowly made my way down an inch at a time on my butt with one of the guides leading the way and my family behind in train formation. Once I was finally able to reach my other daughter who had not bothered venturing up, she looked at me and said, "And *that's* why I stayed here."

It was one thing to have embarrassing things happen around strangers, but it was an even higher level of embarrassment when it happened around people you knew (besides immediate family). This brought me to the school incident. Again, being the loving mom that I was, I was headed to my kids' school to pick them up, but in my slight haste to get there on time, I might have rolled a stop sign just before the school parking lot. As luck would have it, a police officer witnessed this and followed me to the school before having me pull over. Just as the school bell rang, the officer approached me and explained that I had failed to come to a complete stop. Instead of arguing, I simply asked if he could standby (there's that popular flight attendant lingo) for one minute so I could collect my children from the school yard, since they'd be waiting for me and wondering where I was. I was hoping he would just respond with "It's okay, don't worry about it" and let me off with a warning, but instead he chose to graciously wait before dealing out my punishment. When I gathered up my kids, they were surprised to see a police cruiser in the parking lot and were wondering who was going to get in trouble. "He's here for me," I told them and then watched as their mouths dropped.

My brush with the law came into play yet again, this time after one of my flights. I had just returned from a long winter turnaround and was looking forward to a relaxing car ride home. I blasted my heat, turned on my radio, and off I went. As you might recall, flatulence was a major thing when flying. On this day, I had chosen to be the martyr and instead of having my passengers and fellow crew suffer on board, I self-sacrificed and saved my gas for the privacy of my own car. I was tooting along singing to the tunes (of the radio, not my toots) when I noticed a random roadside spot check on the ramp to the highway. My singing abruptly stopped when I quickly realized what was about to happen. The spot checks were purposely situated so that once you saw them, there was no backing out. I was stuck. I rolled down all my windows to try to air out the car, but it was too late. The officer approached my vehicle and shoved his head right up next to me to smell my breath for any alcohol, but instead he was hit by my toxic fumes. Mortified couldn't even begin to describe how I felt. At least when my husband farted in our apartment's elevator at 0300 hours thinking no one else would be riding with us at that unfortunate time, he could blame it on me.

My embarrassing moments felt like they doubled in their humiliation impact when I was dressed in uniform. I didn't even have to be on the aircraft yet before I would do something that made my face turn red. When I arrived at my gate for one early morning turn, I walked past the boarding counter and through the locked doors that led to the bridge. Normally there would be a ground agent who would greet me there and sometimes even open the door, but since I was early, I didn't think anything of it and proceeded to let myself in. I knew what the code for the doors was, but I must have pressed a wrong number because when I attempted to push it open, alarm bells started blaring. Naturally everyone in the lounge area looked over at me and any babies who were sleeping were now awake. I quickly punched in the numbers again to stop the alarm, hoping this time I did it correctly. Thankfully it worked, and I bolted to the bridge so I would be out of sight. It was a fairly long bridge that curved around, so I didn't realize until I had reached the end that there was no plane and nowhere to go. I sprinted back hoping no one would see me on the bridge that led nowhere but unfortunately that wasn't the case. When I reached back to the start, the captain was already there.

"No plane, huh?" he asked, knowing very well that it hadn't arrived yet.

If I wasn't in such a hurry to head onto the bridge and out of passenger sight, I would have looked out the window and clearly seen the spot where the plane should have been, was vacant.

The embarrassments I seemed to attract were not reserved solely for those on the ground either. I made a good effort not to deprive my fellow air travellers as well. There were the little incidents, such as doing a whole beverage service with my pants zipper down or having a sesame seed caught in my front teeth. This would be after scarfing down half a turkey sandwich in between services because I was starving and still hadn't had my break. There was also the time I had to wrap my shoe with duct tape to hold the sole on even though they were newly purchased. As a side note, duct tape was a very versatile tool on the aircraft used to fix armrests, bins, lav doors, and even very talkative people, as demonstrated by a captain when he used it on a first officer. The upside of working in the cabin versus in the cockpit was that we got to socialize with different passengers and crew members; whereas the pilots only had each other for the majority of the flight. Some pilots had a very outgoing personality and enjoyed talking—a lot—while others preferred more of a talk-to-me-when-you-need-me attitude. On this day, the captain was the latter and jokingly placed a piece of duct tape over the first officer's mouth as his "subtle" way of telling him to stop talking (as told by the first officer when he exited the cockpit to use the lavatory and was questioned by the flight director why his mouth was covered).

Then there were the larger, more embarrassing incidents that I experienced in flight. This specific embarrassment ended with me in tears (yet again). This time, though, it was over wasabi and not my fear of heights, and yes, I recognized the irony here. We had recently started selling California rolls on board and, having never tried wasabi before, I decided to put one of these rolls aside to try during my break. We finished our services with ease, and I had a little bit of time to myself, so I sat down in an empty passenger row at the aft of the aircraft and opened my package. I was excited to try something new. Not knowing anything about wasabi etiquette, I emptied the entire package onto one roll. Anyone who has never eaten wasabi before—don't do this! The package should have come with a warning: only consume a miniscule amount at once or you will die. I died. My eyes burst wide open as fire consumed my mouth. I was hacking and crying and putting on a real good spectacle of myself, and yet no one came to my aid! The attention I seemed to have drawn was that of annoyance instead of sympathy. *Sorry I interrupted your movie. I'll go back to dying quietly now.*

The instances when I could simply stand back and observe awkward situations happening to other flight attendants were far more enjoyable than being the victim myself. We had just taken off and were in the middle of our first service in which we sold blankets and headsets as well as handed out complimentary kids' bags and headsets to passengers under twelve. My colleague was working the opposite side of the double trolley with me when she passed a kid's bag to a passenger. It turned out this "kid" was a thirty-year-old little person. He was a good sport about it and laughed it off, but my colleague was mortified. Her face had gone beet red and she could not stop apologizing.

This was similar to the time I asked a passenger what her age was when she was seated in the emergency exit row (you had to be at least sixteen years old to sit there), and she said she was twenty-four. Or the time I called a passenger *sir* instead of *miss*. The times we'd mistaken ages and sexes were always embarrassing but unfortunately were still common occurrences.

Being a flight attendant, I knew I was bound to run into someone I knew on a flight sooner or later. This happened quite a few times for me over the years. My former nurse who used to give me weekly allergy shots when I was a kid, had recognized me on one of my flights. After twenty years, I guess I still looked like that nine-year-old girl with pigtails. I had run into a former high school French teacher, a teacher from my kids' school, an old co-worker from a previous job, my children's friends' families, and so on. You got the idea. This was all fine, since we liked one another, and we were genuinely happy to catch up. The problem arose when it was someone I preferred never to see again.

On the outbound portion of this particular day, I was kneeling down while stuffing hot casseroles into a trolley, and at the same time, another flight attendant decided to pull out a retractable ledge right over my head without my knowledge. As I went to stand, I banged my forehead directly into the side of this ledge, leaving me with a small cut and a nasty bump. My colleagues quickly passed me some ice to apply, but it had already turned into an ugly sight. It was directly in the centre of my forehead so that no one could miss it. At any rate we landed, said goodbye to our passengers, and prepared the plane for the return flight.

We were using two sets of doors to board the plane that day, and my partner in the aft was supposed to be responsible for that position, but he was still busy preparing items in the galley when the passengers were arriving and asked if I could assist. Not a problem. One by one I checked the passengers' boarding cards and told them which way it was to their seats. Then before even looking up, I heard the passenger now standing in front of me call out my name. Of course, it had to be none other than my ex. And here I was with this big-ass bulge radiating off my shiny forehead. I put on my fake smile and pretended like I didn't remember that last time we had seen each other. I believe my exact words were "fuck you," just before storming out of a café. Six years later, here we were. As it turned out, he was still single while I was now happily married with a beautiful baby girl. *Ha!* I was feeling good about myself again, and then he asked me what happened to my head.

Unfortunately, that shadow of embarrassment also followed me abroad. While on a layover in London, I hadn't been feeling well and because my husband and I had been doing more than talking about starting a family, I thought I'd satisfy my curiosity and buy a pregnancy test from Boots (UK's equivalent to Canada's Shopper's Drug Mart). Back alone in my hotel room I carefully followed the instructions and anxiously awaited the results. The stick confirmed my suspicions, and I was indeed pregnant. I was elated and nervous at the same time. It all felt so bittersweet because I couldn't wait to share the news with my husband, but I didn't want to tell him over the phone. I wanted to see his reaction in person. The next day, while we were boarding the aircraft for my flight back home, I was still feeling nauseous. One of my colleagues thought I was sick and asked if there was anything she could do for me. I confided in her that I just found out I was pregnant—big mistake. After the flight director made her welcome announcement, she took the opportunity to announce my pregnancy over the intercom to the entire plane, asking everyone to welcome her in congratulating me. I was so embarrassed. Here I was, a nauseous introvert now having to thank complete strangers for their well wishes. More than three hundred random people now knew my great news before my own husband.

During another layover in London, the crew and I had arrived at the hotel, were given our room keys, and as per the norm, everyone split. I decided to stick around for the convenience store in the lobby to open since the sign said BACK IN 5 MINUTES, and I needed some feminine hygiene products. (Aunt Flow had inconveniently decided she would tag along on my layover at the last minute.) One hour later I awoke to find myself still in the lobby but now slouched over on the bench with drool flowing down my chin. The girl behind the check-in counter was looking at me pitifully. With impressionable speed I composed myself, swiped the drool off my face, grabbed my bags, and ran straight for the elevators. Aunt Flow would have to wait because my only thought now was to exit the lobby immediately.

Unlike many of the other flight attendants, I usually preferred venturing out without napping when arriving at a layover. It was a beautiful day in Rome, and so I decided I would take a stroll through a park I hadn't been to before. Of course, I inevitably got a little lost, and three hours later, I eventually found my way back towards the hotel. By this point I was hot, my legs were shaking, and I more than surely resembled a zombie. One second I was walking, and the next I was performing what I liked to call a Superman-splat. It was like one of those slow-motion action scenes you saw in the movies. I could see it happening but couldn't do anything to prevent it. The cobblestone from under my feet leapt up and tripped me. And I flew—literally. My arms went flailing in the air and then *splat*! I was flat on my belly with my face to the sidewalk. And just to add insult to injury, my graceful fall was witnessed by everyone sitting at the sidewalk café. And who should come to my rescue? None other than an elderly couple. Figures.

A friend of mine once shared an embarrassing moment she had on a layover in London that also involved an elderly couple. She had checked into the hotel, gotten her key, and entered her room. She urgently needed to use the toilet, so she rolled her luggage into the room and immediately slipped into the bathroom. For lack of better words, she took a noisy, nasty poop, washed her hands, and exited the bathroom now half dressed. She proceeded to push her luggage into the room to unpack, and that's when she saw them. An elderly couple was lying in the bed with the sheets pulled right up to their heads. They had been too afraid to move not knowing who had entered their room. My friend was extremely embarrassed and left as fast as she could get herself re-dressed while at the same time apologizing to the couple. She said she didn't know whether she felt worse for almost giving this poor old couple a heartache or for the nasty stink she left in their bathroom.

Sometimes I wondered if the embarrassments just reared their ugly heads as an act of karma, like the time I was on a layover in Cancun. My colleague chose to ignore my warning that the ocean waves seemed too strong to go swimming. She was about the size and weight of my pool noodle, and so sure enough, she was knocked over by the first wave that hit her. Not only did the ocean knock her down to her knees, but it also slapped and tossed her back and forth like a defenseless little rag doll. Once I managed to get enough video and restrain my laughter, I helped her out of the water, and we continued the rest of the day by the pool.

As karma would have it, the next time I returned to Cancun and forgot to pack sunscreen, resulting in a colleague lending me her sun tanning oil, I was due for an embarrassment of my own. Please note, sunscreen and sun tanning oil were not the same, especially on a fair-skinned-prone-to-burning person like me. Needless to say, my legs were charred. It was like my honeymoon all over again, except that time I naively thought the shade from a tree would protect me. I guess you could safely say that the sun and I did not have a particularly good relationship, which was probably why I was one of those few flight attendants who preferred layovers in rainy, cloudy cities like London or Glasgow.

Whether it was on vacations, at home, at the airport, on flights, or while on layovers, embarrassments had a way of following me. They were my shadow that lingered even when the sun had disappeared. I guess for every time I laughed at others, including the countless snoring passengers, it was only fitting that Miss Karma would be dishing out embarrassments on me. Unfortunately for me, she has barely cracked the surface.

Chapter Eleven

The Layovers

One of the best perks of being a flight attendant was not only being able to visit so many different cities around the world (or at least wherever my airline flew) but also getting paid doing so. In the beginning it felt surreal as I would tour around admiring everything each city had to offer me as a first-time tourist. After many repeated visits of the same city, however, I would start to settle in and begin acting more like a local. Now it was all about shopping, food, and sleep.

My very first layover with my company was to London, England. I had never been there before and was excited to see everything the city had to offer, except by the time I got there, I was so tired that I needed to sleep. I didn't see any of the main tourist attractions, such as Buckingham Palace or Big Ben, because my only priority after I woke from my nap was to get something to eat. I knew I'd be back again anyway, so it wasn't a big deal. Just being able to walk around in a city where everyone drove on the opposite side, spoke with a cool accent, and offered stores and foods I had never seen before were plenty enough for my first time travelling alone. (Thank goodness for the signs they had painted on their sidewalks at most main intersections that said Look Right or Look Left.) I walked for over an hour, grabbed a bite to eat, and then was ready to return to the hotel. I didn't want to have to walk all the way back, so I decided to catch a bus. This would be the start of my getting lost while on a layover.

After I had my fill of touring the various locations I had been interested in seeing, such as Paris, Barcelona, Athens, Amsterdam, Frankfurt, Brussels, Lisbon, and various places in the UK (I had already seen Italy and Switzerland by this point, so these had already been checked off my list.), I started requesting destinations according to the needs in my kitchen. If I were in France, for example, I could purchase some of the most amazing cheeses and macarons. There were so many different shop options, I made sure to try different ones each time. Unfortunately, bringing back cheese also made for a stinky return flight. I always knew when a colleague was getting ice from the canister where I'd store my cheese because the smell would increase substantially.

Since I cooked a lot of Italian dishes, Italy had quite a few options for me, including polenta, arborio rice, balsamic vinegar, dried pasta, and Parmesan cheese. Nutella and sweets, such as biscotti and cannoli, were a must, and of course I could never forget the coffee.

Portugal was where I discovered *pastéis de nata*. They were these little pastry tarts filled with custard that were crispy on the outside and full of heaven on the inside. They were so good that I bought a dozen to bring home with me the first time I ever had one. (A dozen did not make it all the way home by the way.)

Scotland was where I would stock up on those seasoning cooking bags. The ones in which you basically just added some chicken in a pre-seasoned bag and threw it into the oven. They had a ton of varieties for super cheap. I could also never return from Scotland without their shortbread. I especially loved dunking it into the coffee from Italy.

England provided me with clotted cream, sweets, such as Cadbury chocolates and Percy Pigs (pig-shaped soft candy), as well as amazing scones. I would request these fresh from the baker and then buy as many as were available to me so that I could freeze some once I got home and even share with my mother-in-law who also really enjoyed them.

Although I never bothered bringing back olive oil, many of my colleagues and passengers would do so when returning from either Italy, Spain, or Greece. Wine was also something my colleagues enjoyed bringing home, especially from France, Italy, Spain, Portugal, Greece—from anywhere really. I preferred to leave my drinking in the past (or in Barcelona), and so I never purchased any alcohol to bring home.

From kitchen staples to world-famous culinary delights, each layover destination really did offer magnificent foods that I found simply irresistible, such as the chocolate crepes of Paris found on just about every corner and made in any number of ways. And who could resist their baguettes? They were so fresh and crunchy, and you didn't even have to put anything in them to enjoy. It was common to see people picnicking with their baguettes on the lawn near the Eiffel Tower.

When in Italy, pizza was a must. Italian pizza was oven baked with a super thin crust. When ordering a pizza, you would be served an entire one for yourself. This might seem daunting at first, but trust me, that whole pizza would not go to waste. Do not ask for pepperoni topping, though, unless you wanted hot dog pieces because that was exactly what you would get. Arugula topping was a popular choice and oddly enough, very tasty on a pizza. My personal favourite tended to be any meat with onion and arugula (just not horse meat).

If you happened to be in Italy during the fall season, that was when you'd notice many of the street vendors selling *castagne*. These were roasted chestnuts that were in high demand during chestnut season in Italy. When I'd be out for a stroll in the evenings, a nice bag of warm nuts would be very yummy and comforting. (Okay, stop the giggling.) Then there were the coffee and desserts. A cappuccino with a side of cannoli. Yes, please!

Frankfurt was the city of apple strudel and schnitzel. You've probably eaten these elsewhere already, but no one could do strudel and schnitzel justice like Germany could. I was excited when my family and I had a fourteen-hour stopover here on our way to Africa so that they could try these delicious foods. We took the train from the airport to central Frankfurt, but everywhere we tried, they either weren't serving it or had run out. We ended up eating bison burgers instead, which were surprisingly tasty.

Unfortunately, I did not spend too much time in Athens, but the little I was there I can say their gyros and baklava were amazing. One time I was only there for a total of nine hours and ended up eating Ben and Jerry's ice cream from the store in the hotel lobby before falling asleep and then having to leave again.

The thing about being a flight attendant with my airline was that you had to get around to seeing certain destinations fairly quickly because they could be around one year and the next, they'd no longer be available as a layover. I was happy I was able to see places like Brussels and Shannon, for instance, because otherwise I never would have seen the Manneken Pis, which was a lot smaller than I had expected the statue to be, or suggested to my husband that we name our firstborn Shannon .

Depending on where I was headed for my layover, I usually knew what I could expect. If I was staying in central London, I would bring along my running shoes because I knew I would want to go for a jog through Hyde Park and Kensington Gardens. Jogging through Dublin's St. Stephen's Green was also enjoyable, but because it wasn't excessively big, I'd find myself lapping around the park and then continuing the jog down along River Liffey. If I was staying anywhere that was too hot to jog outside, I'd just go for a long walk instead. Sometimes I'd use the treadmill in the hotel's gym, but I found them to be too boring and I wasn't that dedicated of a runner anyway.

Another thing I could be sure to expect on certain layovers was getting lost. No matter how many times I'd stay in certain places, getting lost seemed to be my specialty. Venice was notorious for having me walk in circles. There were so many little alleys and bridges that after a while all started to look the same. Following the many signs on the buildings didn't help either, as they would point in multiple directions, and then it was up to me to decide which arrow to follow.

On one of my Venice layovers my colleague and I both decided we'd bring our daughters along. Since our kids already knew each other and were close in age, we thought it would be fun if we all spent the day together. My eldest daughter was seventeen at the time, my middle daughter fourteen, and my colleague's daughter twelve, so we knew they could handle a twenty-four-hour layover in

Venice as long as they promised to sleep on the plane. It was to be a girls' weekend adventure. We had gelato—a must in Italy. My favourites would have to be lemon, pistachio, and chocolate hazelnut. We took pictures with pigeons at the Piazza San Marco, shared a gondola ride on the Grand Canal (my friend rejected the first gondolier offered to us because he wasn't cute enough, but the wait was worth it), walked the Rialto Bridge, shopped in the alley stores, and then finished off with a delicious dinner at an outdoor restaurant. We had all enjoyed a very pleasant day in Venice, but then it was time to catch the bus back to our hotel. This is where things took a turn.

We attempted to follow the signs accordingly but after going through a maze of alleys and circling around squares, we eventually found ourselves at a deadlock. We either had the choice of scaling a building or swimming across a canal. We chose neither and instead began to backtrack, which was when we came across another couple who had apparently followed the same signs as we did and were headed to the same deadlock we were at. After much frustration we eventually found ourselves at the bus station—exhausted. As we sat on the bus in silence, hair frizzy from the humidity, I thought, *at least our gondolier was cute.*

Amsterdam was another city that always seemed to cause me a directional challenge. The first time I ever went to De Wallen (the infamous Red Light District) was completely by accident. I was trying to find my way back to the hotel after taking a self-tour of the city but somehow managed to take a wrong turn and didn't know where I was until I noticed all the sex shops, peep shows, and cannabis cafés. *My husband would love it here.* I ultimately learned that as long as I could find Amstel, the main river, I could eventually find my hotel. On one of my layovers here I found myself walking with an elderly couple after they stopped to ask *me* for directions, and it turned out we were both trying to make our way to Amstel.

When my friend and I decided we would both bring our daughters along on a different layover the following year, we chose Scotland. (This time I only brought my middle daughter along because my eldest was "busy," but I did end up bringing her to Scotland with me the next year, and her sister again, because it was now her favourite place.) We spent our first day in Glasgow and the next in Edinburgh. We each took our daughters around Glasgow on our own and then met up for dinner. I brought my daughter to Glasgow Greens, where we saw the People's Palace and the Winter Gardens and then walked along River Clyde. Her favourite however, was the shopping. Glasgow offered many shopping opportunities, and she certainly took full advantage of it.

The next morning my friend and I took our daughters to Edinburgh via the train. I absolutely loved Edinburgh and was excited to show the girls all it had to offer. We went to the National Museum of Scotland, where we saw Dolly (the cloned sheep), and took in a view of the city from its rooftop terrace. Then we took pictures in front of The Elephant House. This was where J.K. Rowling sat and wrote much of her *Harry Potter* novels. Right next door was Greyfriars Kirkyard, a graveyard where the same author found her inspiration in naming some of her *Harry Potter* characters, including the popular Thomas Riddell (a.k.a. Lord Voldemort). As we made our way towards Edinburgh Castle, we walked along Victoria Street, which was a curving cobbled street resembling *Harry Potter*'s Diagon Alley. (If you were a *Harry Potter* fan, Edinburgh was a must.) This was when we became a little disoriented.

It should have been a quick jaunt to Edinburgh Castle from there but instead we ended up taking more of a scenic route. We decided to cave and finally ask for directions, and consequently we managed to arrive at the castle. After taking in all the views, which included the guards in their kilts, we walked a wee bit of the Royal Mile before making our way to the Royal Botanic Garden by taxi. Incidentally, my daughter decided right then and there that this would be the place where she would one day wed. On our return the taxi driver dropped us off on Princes Street, where we let our girls bask in more shopping. Besides the small hiccup when trying to find the castle, we had fared relatively well with directions that day, that is until we chose to visit Holyrood Palace after some more shopping.

Had we known the Royal Mile from the castle led directly to the palace, we probably would have continued on that path when we were there earlier. At any rate, after much unnecessary walking from poor directions, we found ourselves at the base of some cool-looking cliffs. We took one of the paths provided and proceeded to climb upward. I later discovered that we were on Salisbury Crags, just west of the palace. When we rounded a corner, we saw there was a gathering of people and a fire burning. We joined the other spectators and enjoyed the view from the top of a cliff (okay, the girls did while I remained farther down in a more secured area). The firefighters informed us that all they could do was simply watch that the grass fire, which had broken out, didn't spread any farther and so others, too, seemed to all join the watch. The current fire prevented us from going any farther on our upward trek as they had roped off the path leading to Arthur's Seat. (I didn't mind this in the least.) Now that we knew where Holyrood Palace was exactly, we had no difficulty in finding it and concluding our tour of Edinburgh. What I learned from this was that getting lost sometimes paid off, as we saw things that we never would have planned otherwise.

Fire at Salisbury Crags

Other times getting lost was only plain frustrating. When I took the subway in Lisbon, I was expecting it to be more straightforward. I had taken the underground in London, the subways in New York City, and the metro in Paris, so how hard could it be? I don't know if it was because I was tired or because I couldn't speak Portuguese, but I ended up going in the opposite direction of where I intended before realizing it and having to turn back again. At least I ate some good food. This was the day I first tried *bife a portuguesa*. This was simply steak and egg Portuguese style, which seemed odd together until I tried it and was delightfully surprised.

When I was out jogging in Dublin, I decided to take a different route than the one I was used to because it was a beautiful day and I felt like exploring new sites.

What I didn't count on was adding on so many extra kilometers to my run because my sense of direction kept leading me further away instead of circling me back to the hotel as I had hoped. Many of the street names were either missing or well-hidden on the sides of buildings so it was difficult to get my bearings. After a few failed attempts down different roads and eventually asking strangers for directions, I managed to make my way back. I was sweaty and exhausted but, on a positive note, I did see some nice scenery.

Unless I was bringing family along, if I were in a previously visited city I would typically wander around on my own and then possibly meet up for dinner with the crew. It was common for crew to do their own thing and then meet up later so there was never any pressure to hang out on layovers. There was no expectation for the crew to even have dinner together. Whoever wanted to go, would show up at a pre-determined time, and whoever didn't or changed their mind, no big deal. Sometimes though I'd meet up with a colleague before dinner for some aperitifs. (As long as we didn't consume any alcohol twelve hours before duty, we were free to drink.) Such was the case in Barcelona where the sangria was found in abundance. My friend and I shared a pitcher of this delicious traditional punch-type wine at a sidewalk café near our hotel, and before we knew it, it was already time to meet our other friend for dinner. Just as I was thinking we should finish up, our friend walked past on her way to meet us at the restaurant but hadn't noticed us still at the café. We tried to yell out to her, but she didn't hear us, so I attempted to run towards her except the second I stood, my legs buckled, and I had to sit back down. "Oh well, we tried," I said to my friend as we continued drinking.

Me with my personal pitcher of yummy sangria in Barcelona

Apparently drinking half a pitcher of sangria on an empty stomach wasn't the brightest idea, but it sure was good. Since we had accidentally ditched our friend for dinner and we were both a little wobbly, we figured we'd go somewhere closer to eat dinner. That was when my friend introduced me to foie gras. I didn't know what it was, so she simply explained that it was like cheese. I thought it sounded like awfully expensive cheese, but I was always willing to try something at least once, so we split on an order. I didn't particularly care for it, but I ate it anyway. While I was eating it, however, she seemed to have that familiar look my mother gave me as a kid when we were in Italy and she tricked me into eating *carne equina* (horse meat). My suspicions were right. I had eaten the liver of a force-fed duck. *More sangria, please!*

Sometimes when I had a layover with someone I really meshed well with, I would venture out with them even if it were somewhere I had already been to or seen over a dozen times. When I was in Rome, a colleague and I decided to take a stroll around the crowded cobblestone streets of the major tourist areas such as the Coliseum, Trevi Fountain, and the Spanish Steps. We enjoyed a gelato and a cappuccino before heading back to the hotel to freshen up for dinner. A simple *"passeggiata"* – leisurely stroll - in good company was always enjoyable.

Once I had exhausted the sightseeing that certain cities had to offer and my kitchen was well stocked, I would usually turn to Glasgow as my preferred choice since it tended to be cool and overcast. I knew where all the hotspots were for free Wi-Fi, and if the complimentary city connection was good, I would even FaceTime with my family while walking downtown. Strolling along the streets and through the stores of Glasgow was the perfect me time where nobody knew or bothered me. Except when I went into one of those stores once only to run into a couple of passengers who were on my flight over.

"Hey, remember us?" the man asked.

Nope, I was about to answer when his wife pulled him away telling him to leave me alone because I probably had had enough of him from the flight. God bless her.

I didn't usually go out for dinner with others in Glasgow. I was comfortable ordering from a familiar Thai restaurant and then returning to my hotel room to eat in front of the television. Like I said, me time. Sometimes I preferred Delsey dining* and wouldn't even have to purchase any food. These were usually the times when I was either on a health kick and was watching everything I was eating or when I was being frugal and didn't want to spend any of my per diem.

Even though I enjoyed having time to myself and occasionally dining with colleagues, I still also enjoyed bringing my family along on layovers. The first— and last— time I brought my entire family with me on a layover was when we stayed in Amsterdam for forty-eight hours. We all went to the Anne Frank House and the Van Gogh Museum, and then while my eldest daughter and I went to see exhibitions of artists, such as Andy Warhol and Banksy, the rest of my family chose to wait in the square by the Rijksmuseum. We sat on the bench from *The Fault in Our Stars* movie, ate some of the best fries, watched a virtual reality movie, and made sure not to get in the way of the insane number of bicyclists as we wandered the streets. To end our stay in Amsterdam we dined in a restaurant, where my children watched a couple make out at a nearby table. As much as I appreciated having my whole family with me, it was much easier only taking one or two of them at once. This way I could spend less money, have fewer arguments, and have more room in my hotel room.

The first date night I had with my husband on a layover was in Venice for twenty-four hours. We enjoyed pizza and gelato together while our kids enjoyed freebase* for the first time. This was their test. If the house was still standing and everyone, including the dog, was still alive, we would consider allowing them further freebases in the future. They went above and beyond to secure their future freedom. The house was spotless, everyone was happy and safe, and our neighbour who we entrusted to spy on the kids said he only had to call the cops once (wink). For my next date-night layover, my husband and I left for forty-eight hours. We doubled our kids' freedom time and once again, it was a success. Long gone were the days of having to trek around strollers and baby diapers.

My daughter, Shannon, falling asleep on our train ride from Edinburgh to Glasgow. (Not everyone is cut out to be a flight attendant.)

Since I had already taken my daughters on a couple of layovers with me, including to Venice and Glasgow, it was only fair that I took my son as well. After taking him to Venice, where I treated him to a gondola ride, pizza, and gelato, he decided he preferred to stay home. At least this time, thanks to the water bus, I didn't get lost. My son's favourite memory of Venice was the banana milkshake from McDonald's. I guess it was safe to say he was a little spoiled. In fact, his look of disbelief when taking his economy seat on our long route to Africa was priceless. "What is this?" I heard him mutter before wedging himself into his seat.

My son, Adam, enjoying his spacious seat back from Venice.

Once arriving at a layover destination, collecting my luggage (if I had checked any), and going through customs, I would then make my way to the crew pick-up area, where hopefully our transportation would already be there. The unfortunate times it was not and the crew had to wait was extremely aggravating, since this just meant an even longer time before being able to rest and decontaminate. Once on the bus, or sometimes van, it could either be a quick fifteen-minute drive or over an hour before arriving at our hotel.

The hotel in Rome was the latter, and so I would take this opportunity to try and get a little shut eye. The key word was *try* because once off the highway the roads were questionable to say the least. The closer we would get to the hotel, the bumpier the roads became. Sleep became impossible as I'd get jostled around. Once we had nearly arrived, I'd be in awe as to how our bus driver was able to weave his way through the tiny cobblestone streets without hitting any of the other vehicles before coming to a stop directly in front of our hotel entrance. If that had been me driving, I would have hit every single car, person, and tree that was two feet too close.

Let me explain. When my husband once came home with a new minivan, I managed to scratch the entire side of it within a week by scraping it along a cart return area when exiting from my parking spot in a plaza. My husband was away on a business trip at the time, so when I called him to let him know that the cart return just jumped right out in front of me, he was not overly impressed. Another day I entered my house with a part of the van's side mirror in hand asking my husband if it could be put back on. It had fallen off when I was backing the van out of the garage. In my defense, it might have been loose. Large vehicles in tight spaces were not my thing. This was the reason why I eventually bought myself Ronald, my small red car.

I was also in awe with a German bus driver the first time I ever had a layover in Frankfurt. It was not due to his driving skills, however, but rather the cooler that he kept next to his seat to share with the crew. When he asked us if we'd like something to drink, I thought he was going to pull out some water, but instead it was a selection of various beers. We accepted his generous offer, and he even shared a beer with us while driving. Frankfurt was already starting to impress me and then I discovered the duvets. The hotel we stayed at had the most amazingly soft duvets I ever had the pleasure of sleeping under. It was like heaven.

Unfortunately, as all good things came to an end, our airline eventually stopped flying to this destination. It was fun while it lasted.

Once I was handed my room key at the hotel, which signified rest time had officially begun, things usually ran smoothly. Even if that hotel was less than a five-star or didn't have motion-sensor faucets. (First-world problems *were* a thing.) The odd time, though, I was given a room that was already occupied. In this case, much like when a passenger would forget to lock the lavatory on the plane, there would be some surprised shrieks followed by a door slam before having to make my way back down to the lobby. There was also a period when fire drills seemed to be common in England. I'm not sure why this was the case as legally they were only required to carry out a fire drill annually (more if there was a high turnover in staff). Maybe it was just my dumb luck to be staying at certain hotels on fire drill day. As much as I wanted to ignore the loud dinging, it was impossible, and I would end up leaving the building, not because I thought there was a fire, but because the alarm was so loud and irritating.

Usually, the hotel would inform us if they expected any drills or maintenance to occur while we were there. This wasn't the case, however, the day I woke from a nap only to find a window washer directly outside my window. I now always close the curtains once inside my room. Aside from the odd inconveniences, my hotel stays were uneventful.

Except the time I brought my father along. He hadn't seen his twin brother for seven years, so I thought it would be nice to bring my dad on a layover to Venice with me while his brother could drive the approximate three-hour journey from Como to meet us. From the moment we were handed our room key we had issues. First off, the swipe card to enter our room wouldn't work, so back down we trekked with our luggage in tow to inquire about this dilemma. When we were assured it was fixed, we returned to the room and proceeded to unpack and freshen up so we could then meet up with my uncle.

My dad with the "exploding" sink in our hotel room in Venice.

As I was unpacking, I heard a bang and some Italian swear words coming from the bathroom. I quickly ran to see what was going on and found my dad trying to replace the tap, which had exploded off the sink leaving water spraying everywhere. He had been attempting to shave but instead he took an unexpected shower. Being the handyman that he was, my dad managed to turn off the water and replace the tap while I sopped up the water. Luckily, the bathroom had two sinks, so we just carried on and made a mental note not to use the broken one again. Then it was my turn to get ready. I decided to take a quick shower, but once finished I realized there was no bath towel. We had used the spare hand towels to dry up the explosion but never noticed that there were no bath towels. I yelled out to my father, who then called maid service so we could finally finish getting ready.

My uncle had driven in from Como with my aunt and another couple who were long-time friends of my dad's, and we enjoyed the rest of the day catching up. After saying our farewells, my dad and I went for dinner together and then retired back to our room for a good night's sleep. Normally I liked to watch television before falling asleep because I found it relaxing, but I became somewhat irritated when I saw that it was only facing the sitting area, which was behind the wall to where the bed was. *Whatever.* And so I just went to bed while my dad stayed up a bit longer watching television from the couch. The next morning my father demonstrated the swivel TV wall that he had discovered after I had fallen asleep. All we had to do was rotate the wall to be able to watch television on either side.

Although my dad was clever, he was also forgetful. When I heard Italian swear words coming from the bathroom, I knew he had done it again.

There was no time for jet lag as a flight attendant. Just like the process of settling in at the layover destination, it was simply part of the job. I had no choice but to jump right into the current time zone. I had become accustomed to having to cross several time zones in one day and usually more than once in a week. My greatest number of time zones crossed in one day would have to be when I flew from London to Vancouver, a time difference of eight hours. It was always a treat, however, when the layover was somewhere that either shared the same time zone or was relatively close to home. Montreal, for instance, was like a walk in the park. A quick flight, no time difference, and no money exchange on top of that. The only problem with such a flight, however, was that the pay was significantly less due to the short layover and flight time. I would have enjoyed the Caribbean destinations more if it weren't for the sun and the sand, but I had come to terms with the fact that I wasn't designed for the beach. Calgary, therefore, proved to be fitting. The weather was cool enough to wear my usual jeans and a hoodie. I also didn't have to exchange any money, and the cowboys were easy on the eyes. The first time I had a layover here the crew and I went out to Cowboys Dance Hall. I had no clue how to line dance, but I was willing to give it a whirl. I still couldn't line dance, but I had fun regardless. The next day we went for dinner at a teppanyaki restaurant, which was another first for me, but would certainly not be a last.

Because my husband also travelled quite often for work, we sometimes both found ourselves checking the bed for one another as we slept. He would occasionally get poked in the neck by me while I tended to get whacked in the boob by him. It often felt like a rotating door between the two of us, but at least when he travelled for work, people didn't say, "Have fun on vacation." My job as a flight attendant was anything but a vacation when I was on duty, but I did learn how to make the most of the layovers to see as much of a city in as little time as possible with or without family (if I wasn't lost) and enjoyed the many culinary delights each had to offer. It was not a bad gig to be able to travel the world (or at least where your airline flew) and get paid while doing it.

. . .

*Delsey dining: This is the term used when flight crew eat food they packed in their suitcase rather than buying anything; the Delsey suitcase was later replaced by Samsonite.

*freebase: Not as in smoking crack, but rather this refers to when parents aren't home, and their kids use the opportunity to party.

Chapter Twelve

The Tiredness

Because the fatigue factor was very real in relation to being a flight attendant, it was an important topic to dive deeper into. It was unavoidable and came with the territory of being a flight attendant, regardless of whether you were on a daytime or overnight flight. It not only could affect the crews' own health and well-being but also jeopardize the safety of the passengers on board. Even though there were survival tactics that I used to stay awake and alert, sufficient rest before a flight was still crucial. Unfortunately, tiredness continued to play a major role in explaining a flight attendant's appearance, clumsiness, goofiness, and babbling by the end of some flights.

Flexibility in my sleep pattern was important to achieve the amount of sleep that I required. One day my duty time could be 0500 hours and other days it might not start until 2330 hours. Luckily, I could sleep just about anytime, anywhere. Logically, I found the overnight flights to be the most difficult. It was dark, most of the passengers were sleeping, and I had to stay awake after a whole day at home with my kids and my dog who hadn't allowed me to nap. The crew was allowed a scheduled rest in which short naps were permitted if there was enough flight time remaining. The crew was split so that half would rest while the other half patrolled. By patrolling I mean we were supposed to walk up and down the aisles every so often making sure the passengers were all good, collecting any trash, answering call lights, and checking the lavatories on their cleanliness. What patrolling *truly* meant was having yet another coffee and mingling behind the curtain with the rest of the patrolling crew.

The rest only worked well, however, when crew seats were available. Sitting on a jump seat in front of passengers with closed eyes was not only uncomfortable but also didn't look right. Trying to sit on a jump seat in the galley, besides also being uncomfortable, was noisy and meant being in the way of the other crew who were not resting. Since our aircraft were usually filled, the scheduled rest was therefore not a regular thing. Because our rest times (if any) were relatively short and uncomfortable, I was never able to fall into a deep sleep. By the time I'd grab something to eat, get myself settled, and try to relax, it felt like my eyes would be shut for maybe ten minutes before having to get back to work. Even though I could sleep anywhere, anytime, it would still take me a bit of time to actually fall asleep. I sometimes envied those crew members who could shut their eyes and be dead to the world within a couple of minutes; although, they were also the crabbiest when you'd have to wake them.

Coffee was naturally a must. Some flight attendants became creative with their self-proclaimed concoctions. They were the much appreciated and self-proclaimed flight attendant baristas. Besides coffee, hot water bottles were also an essential item that provided much warmth and comfort on those cold nights. Speaking of which, the coldest areas on a plane tended to be the seats next to an emergency exit door, so if you were going to sit there on an overnight flight, you might want to bring along a hot water bottle as well.

Since our flights were usually so full and we didn't have any seats to sit on besides our jump seats, we'd end up pulling out a canister from a trolley to sit on so we could keep each other awake through galley gatherings of gossip, games, makeovers, and other good stuff. Some of the best company tea was usually spilled during these quiet stretches. This was also where I learned how to twerk and salsa. I still couldn't do either, but I liked to pretend I could just like how my mother used to pretend I could dance when I was a kid. I thought she used to encourage me to continue attending dance lessons because she saw potential, but I found out years later that it was because the lessons were being offered for free, and it gave her time without me at home bugging her. To add to our galley dancing, fog would sometimes get thrown in for effect. This was created by adding hot water to the dry ice we had on hand to keep things cold. Contrary to what many passengers believed, our galleys did not have fridges or microwaves.

The most difficult time when operating an overnight flight while tired had to be sitting on the jump seat just before landing. Knowing we were so close to landing but still having to keep my eyes open and be alert in case of emergency while others around me were just barely opening their eyes proved to be grueling. On one flight, I was seated waiting to land, listening to the passengers directly facing me talk about how much they were missing someone. It sounded like they were talking about their little boy, so when I asked what his name was it turned out it was Bacon, their pet pig. Moments like this, however, helped to keep my eyes open because they were just so bizarre or unusual. By the time we landed at our overseas destination, I would be sleep-deprived, caffeine addicted, and giddy from all the galley gossip, and my words would come out as a mumbled mess. On one of those overnighters, we had arrived in Rome and instead of my usual farewell greetings of "enjoy your vacation" or "thanks for flying with us" or even "goodbye, hope to see you again," I said things like "fun, tanks" and "bye eh." Some passengers just received a head nod along with my squinty red eyes and a couple of giggles.

After an overnight flight, the bus ride to our hotel tended to be incredibly quiet and serene. Simple head nods replaced spoken words. Sunglasses would go on to shield from the rising sun, and it was "Goodnight, Irene." Many flight attendants would give in to their tiredness and choose to take a well-deserved nap when arriving at their hotel before venturing out. I, however, was very stubborn and refused to give in to sleep right away. When I went to bed, I did not want to wake for at least ten hours. My record for longest consecutive uninterrupted sleep was in Paris at sixteen-and-a-half hours. When I eventually woke, I had no idea where I was. This was another common occurrence among flight attendants, since we frequented so many different beds (bad choice of words, but you got what I was trying to say). It was a scary sensation, especially when it was dark, and I couldn't find the darn light and on top of that, my hand was numb because it had still not woken up. Once, when I returned to the hotel after one of my sleep-deprived outings in London, I asked the coffee barista for one last coffee before heading to my room for some shut eye. (I was part Italian—it was normal.) I would never forget his sympathetic look of pity when instead of making me a coffee he leaned over and asked, "Are you okay?" I wanted to cry.

Occasionally, the tiredness would also make its appearance on day flights. Being tired was attributed to much of my clumsiness on board. Dropping pop during a beverage service, for instance, and then serving it to the next passenger because I'd forget I had dropped it was not uncommon for me. This would result in the pop spraying everyone in the vicinity and me offering a free alcoholic beverage or snack so they wouldn't write a complaint. Being a mom, I knew bribes worked. Besides dropping various items, my clumsiness included snagging my clothing more frequently, tripping on nothing specific, and hurting myself more than usual in the galleys. This included burning myself with the ovens, slamming my fingers into the canister doors, or running over my own feet with the trolley. It wasn't unusual for me to give passengers the wrong drink even when I heard it correctly. They might have asked for orange juice, and I'd hand them a coffee, for instance. Sometimes I'd ask what they'd like, turn back to my cart, and have no clue what they just asked for two seconds ago.

When I flew to the Dominican Republic, we had to hand out two different customs and immigration forms to the passengers. One of those forms was to be filled out by every single person, while the other only required one person per household to fill out. On one of those flights, I was so tired that I accidentally reversed the order and handed out the wrong forms. Passengers on my side of the aircraft were left with not enough individual forms and way too many family forms. I had to go back through the aisle and fix my mistake, asking who needed what. Being tired while flying proved to cause extra work. It meant having to sometimes redo services, clean spills, apply first-aid treatment, apologize to—or bribe—passengers, and even repair things.

Fatigue could make you do silly things you normally would not. My colleague shared a time she was on her way home after a flight and needed to quickly run into the store for something. We were not allowed to go shopping while in uniform because it was against company policy to be in uniform anywhere other than for work, so she removed her scarf and wore a coat in her attempt to best cover up and be incognito. Out of her haste and auto-pilot mode she dragged along her company carry-on luggage into the store before realizing what she had done. Tiredness had ratted her out.

As it did to me after one particularly tiring overnight flight. As it turned out, I didn't only cry when scared of heights and eating wasabi; being tired *also* made me cry. I was returning home from an overseas flight and because I was going to land before noon, my family wanted to wait for me so we could go to an amusement park together. That was a mistake. At the top of the roller-coaster ride, I started to cry. My family blamed this on my fear of heights, but I was sure it was the tiredness. I didn't have height issues as long as I was enclosed or strapped into something, which is why I was able to fly on a plane and zip-line without shedding a tear. Unfortunately, the effects of tiredness followed me everywhere.

Survival tactics for tiredness were a necessity whether on a daytime or overnight flight and even off the plane. This probably explains why many flight attendants were coffee addicts. Without adequate sleep, there were inevitable effects on a flight attendant including clumsiness and goofiness but, worst of all, were inattentiveness or carelessness when it came to safety. Getting enough sleep was critical, especially for flight crew who were responsible for the safety of a plane full of passengers. So, if you saw a little curtain wrapped around crew seats, you should never try to peek through and wake the crew attempting to rest. Feel free to bother the others patrolling, however—they might even make you a special coffee if you were lucky.

Chapter Thirteen

The Incidents

Nobody booked a flight with the expectation that a thunderstorm would occur just as your plane was approaching the airport thus causing the pilot to circle for clearance and having to wait, resulting in the plane now running low on fuel and having to divert to another airport instead. As they said, shit happened. As much as airport staff worked tirelessly to ensure everyone's safe travel, sometimes mechanical issues or human error still occurred and other times disasters and mother nature would call the shots.

Even more so than cars, planes underwent maintenance checks to ensure their airworthiness. There were four types of checks, which were known as A-, B-, C-, and D-checks. A-checks were visual routine checks conducted every 120–150 flight hours and would take about eight hours of ground time. B-checks were more detailed checks of components and systems (without any disassembly) and were conducted every 750 flight hours. It took about twenty-four hours of ground time for this check to be completed. C-checks were extensive checks conducted every three thousand flight hours (usually after around twenty-four months). The plane was brought into a hangar and could take anywhere from around five days to one or two weeks for an extensive inspection and therefore would be out of commission during this time. With D-checks, the aircraft was basically stripped to its shell. This check was conducted every twenty thousand flight hours. Aside from these checks, there were various others, such as daily and weekly checks. The pilots also had to adhere to a pre-flight checklist before every flight. This included everything from an exterior walkaround of the aircraft inspecting parts, such as the movement of the flaps, to interior checks, such as testing warning systems.

Sometimes when I would arrive early for my flight and be waiting on the plane, one of the pilots would already be there and have started their checks. Usually, a ground agent or the groomers were there half an hour before the crew was due to arrive, so the bridge and door would already be in place. If no one was there yet, I'd just head back to the gate or wait on the bridge. Sometimes the whole crew would be standing on the bridge going through the pre-flight briefing because the plane might not have arrived at the gate yet. But for the most part, if I was there as early as one of the pilots, I'd see him or her looking out the windows over the wings for snow or frost or I'd hear recorded commands, like "pull-up, pull-up, terrain, terrain," coming from the cockpit. In addition to the maintenance and pilot checks, the aircraft mechanics were always on hand before every flight fixing even the minor repairs, such as a burnt-out reading light or tweaking a latch in the galley, which was also recorded in the logbook.* Despite all these best efforts, however, mechanical issues still arose periodically.

Sometimes mechanicals were minor inconveniences to the flight crew because they would result in an unexpected day at the beach or an extra day on a layover. As long as I wasn't needed back home for anything in particular, they were a welcome and pleasant surprise (emphasis on *welcome*, before I had children). When I operated a turn to Fort Lauderdale I was never expecting to be checking in to a hotel by the beach. It was the same hotel used to film a scene in the movie *Analyze This*, in which mermaids were seen swimming through the windows of the hotel pool behind the bar. Since I was still new to being a flight attendant, I wasn't aware of the need to always pack an emergency bag on a turn. This was a collection of essentials required in case of an unforeseen stay or delay somewhere other than home. It included items such as a change of clothes, shoes, a swimsuit, and toiletries. Along with a couple of other newer crew members during this delay, I went to a beach shop to pick up a few items. I purchased a sundress, a pair of flip-flops, and a couple of other small items before heading to the beach. By late evening the crew received a call from crew sked informing us that the mechanical issue with the aircraft had now been repaired and we would be deadheading back home.

Another time I was having drinks with the crew at our hotel in Amsterdam when the pilot informed us that we were no longer going to be leaving in the morning due to a snowball effect that resulted in our aircraft ending up having to be used elsewhere. We ordered another round.

Although some mechanical delays were at times enjoyable for the crew, other delays were as annoying and inconvenient to us as to the passengers. When I was en route to Rome, we had to first make a stop in Montreal. We embarked some additional passengers and then we were all set to depart again. After pushback the engines were started, and that's when there was a loud bang. The plane came to a stop and the engines were shut down. I sat on my jump seat awaiting instructions. Sure enough, we had to return to the gate, and everyone needed to disembark. The aircraft was deemed unflyable, and the flight was delayed until the next day. The following evening, I still had to operate the same flight with the same passengers to Rome. Once there, however, I would then have to immediately deadhead elsewhere to join another crew in Barcelona and operate back from there instead. The infamous snowball effect had taken its course, and this time it resulted in negative consequences for me as well.

When my grandmother was on her deathbed, my mother went to Italy to be with her, but after a much shorter time than anticipated, my grandmother had sadly passed away. Not wanting to remain there any longer than she needed to, my mother attempted to change her return flight home but was unsuccessful. I had a layover in Frankfurt coming up, so I told my mother to catch a flight there, and we could meet up and stay together and then she could come home on my flight. Everything worked out well, including the crew who was very sympathetic to her. In fact, the captain even offered her a seat in the cockpit for take-off. (This was pre-9/11 when non-flight crew were still permitted in the cockpit.)

Soon after departure I knew something wasn't right. The aircraft did not appear to be climbing but was rather just cruising at a lower altitude. As it turned out, the aircraft was experiencing a pressurization problem and therefore had to remain lower than 10,000 feet. We diverted to Paris and remained on the tarmac for about three hours before repairing the issue and being allowed to depart once again. Just when we thought we were almost home, we had to make an additional fuel stop in Halifax. All I wanted to do was get my poor mom home faster, but instead it had turned into a huge headache. She later informed me that when she was in the cockpit for take-off from Frankfurt, the pilots started speaking French between one another as they were dealing with the problem at hand and then had her exit the cockpit and sit in club class instead. On a positive note, we spent a day in Frankfurt together, she was able to experience sitting in the cockpit, I got her home sooner than originally planned, and it offered her a fair amount of distraction.

Even though human error was unintentional, normal, and a common occurrence, sometimes its results could have detrimental results rather than being simply harmless. Whether it resulted from fatigue, poor training, or speed factors, it did not lessen the severity of the disasters and the accidents that might follow, particularly when it involved a large passenger aircraft. On one of my flights, we had just taken off, and before I knew it our plane was coming back around. Someone from the ground crew had failed to remove the lock safety pins from the landing gear and therefore the pilots were unable to retract the gear. One of the "remove before flight" items that both ground and flight crews had to physically detach before take-off was ignored. Luckily, this error was easily rectified, and we were on our way once again even though the captain was livid and someone might have gotten fired that day.

When I was working in the lower galley coming back from Gander, the first officer came down the elevator and started checking around the door with his flashlight. He asked if I was hearing any hissing sounds. Apparently when we were in Gander one of the caterers accidentally drove his truck into the side of the plane. I hadn't heard any hissing; however, I felt so much safer after the pilot returned with duct tape in hand. (This is where I'd be eye-rolling.)

Sometimes human error was what preceded new rules being put in place to prevent further similar actions from occurring. Rules, such as not taking any feet off the plane to close cabin doors so as not to fall onto the tarmac or cross checking the unarming of doors to not pop a slide, were therefore imposed at my company. As much as imposing rules helped, human error occurred regardless but hopefully only resulted in minor inconveniences. So, when the ground staff brought the wrong stairs to the aircraft or the new guy positioned the bridge incorrectly or the luggage handler lost your bag, just be happy you arrived safely.

Disasters were thankfully nothing I ever had to experience personally, unless you counted epidemics, such as SARS and COVID-19, and even then, it was short-lived. I was on maternity leave during the worst part of the SARS epidemic, and so I only experienced the tail end of it. Shared items on board, such as pillows and blankets, were no longer being provided and hand sanitizing was highly recommended. When the COVID-19 outbreak occurred, I volunteered in the repatriation flights until our aircraft were forcibly grounded.* During these flights, I had to wear a face mask and gloves, and our services were limited to pre-packaged items only. The passengers were extremely grateful just to get home safe.

The 9/11 tragedy was by far the greatest disaster the airline industry had ever faced. Like everyone else who was old enough to remember, I knew exactly what I was doing when the whole world stopped on September 11, 2001. While on a leave of absence from work due to my second miscarriage, I was on my way to my friend's house with my one-year-old daughter. I had the radio on as I was driving when the song playing was interrupted by an important announcement. When I first heard the news of an airplane crashing into the World Trade Center, I thought it was odd. Around fifteen minutes later I had just arrived at my friend's place when another announcement came on the radio to say a second airplane had crashed into the same building. This was when I knew something was terribly wrong. I went up to my friend's apartment and told her to turn the television on. She still hadn't heard the news as we both watched in disbelief. My heart went out to everyone who was ever affected by these horrendous attacks.

Because commercial airliners were used as weapons by the terrorists in the attacks, 9/11 changed the airline industry forever. Extensive security precautions were put in place, which included stricter airport screening and tighter control. It became standard for cockpit doors to be bulletproof and locked at all times during the flight, and passengers were no longer allowed in. Some aircraft had cameras installed so that the pilots could view the cabin. Flight crew were also given additional training pertaining to the security of the aircraft, particularly the cockpit. When I returned to work after the attacks, it felt like a much more cautious environment. Many were still afraid to travel, but those who did were faced with longer wait times as they were subjected to more thorough checks than had been the norm prior to this. On the aircraft I had to get used to saying no to the children who wanted to visit the cockpit during the flight as well as having to request permission from the pilots to unlock the door so that I could enter. It was a new world in aviation but one that everyone would soon enough become accustomed to.

No one could mess with mother nature. Whether she chose to unleash a snowstorm or simply blow some extra wind our way, many times she held the deciding vote in the fate of our flight. Winter flying was always the worst, which was why I would try to take as much vacation time over the winter months as I could. Delays and cancellations were frequent occurrences. Even door issues would arise due to frozen locks. It was not uncommon to rush the boarding so we could quickly push back and join the line at the de-icing pad. It was first come, first served so the faster we could get there, the quicker we could depart. It wasn't unheard of to have the departure lineup so backed up that by the time it was our turn for take-off, we had to de-ice again.

If there was too much snow accumulation, flights were either delayed or cancelled, as the ground staff worked feverishly to clear the runways. As I was waiting for my plane to arrive at the gate on one icy, cold morning, I looked outside and watched as the luggage cart being driven was sliding around on the tarmac and nearly hit a plane. I knew it was going to be a long and trying day at that point.

On my return from London one year, I was sitting on the crew bus with my colleagues as we awaited our aircraft to arrive, and while waiting, we watched the ground staff struggle with snow removal. It was evident that they weren't used to dealing with snow there. They were loading snow onto a dump truck, but they didn't realize the snow was falling out from the flap on the back side at the same time. It reminded me of when I was in Zimbabwe with my family and they had us shovel sand onto a flatbed truck. Not only was the sand going over the sides of the truck but also through the wooden slats. They were so spaced apart that we would watch the sand fall from underneath as we threw more on. All our hard work was literally escaping. It took a lot of effort before we were able to accumulate a fair amount of sand. Even the cows that ended up surrounding us found it entertaining. We were jokingly told by the locals that Zimbabweans were hard workers not smart workers.

My three children shovelling sand onto the truck in Zimbabwe. (Notice the sand falling through the slats?)

The worst flying conditions were probably during periods of heavy snow or hail, but thunderstorms could be just as troubling for departures and arrivals. If we were already in the air, the pilots could usually fly around it thereby not causing much, if any, disruption. The problem arose on landing if the airport had been temporarily closed. As we'd be approaching, the pilot would be told to either slow down or remain in a holding pattern* until receiving clearance to land. If the storm persisted, we would eventually have to divert to an alternative, nearby airport to refuel and wait it out. On one of my flights back from Punta Cana, the flight director informed the rest of the crew that the pilots were attempting to slow our approach into YYZ because there were thunderstorms in the area and the airport had been shut down temporarily. The captain was hoping that by the time we were nearly there, the thunderstorms would have lifted, and we could land. No such luck. We remained in a holding pattern as long as we could but then had to divert to Hamilton instead because we were now running low on fuel. There was nothing we could do but remain hostage to the weather. The passengers and crew were equally annoyed that we were so close but had no choice to leave. By the time we landed in Hamilton and refuelled, the airport in Toronto had reopened and we could now land—two hours later. It was like the pilot playing a cruel game and saying "Psych!" just before turning the aircraft away from the airport. So close. As scary as lightning sounded, planes were designed and protected against this. I was once sitting in an aircraft on the tarmac when lightning struck, and besides a loud bang and a slight jolt, we were fine. No one except the crew and groomers were on board at the time because we had already disembarked the passengers and still hadn't called for the new ones to come aboard. Besides a couple of people letting out a little shriek from the surprise strike, the day continued as per normal.

Obviously fog caused visibility issues for the pilots, so it, too, could sometimes cause delays, as we would have to wait for it to lift before being able to depart. Overheating was an issue if on the ground with the passengers for too long with no air conditioning at a hot or humid destination. If unable to use the auxiliary power unit when boarding in a hot location, we would close all the window shades and request to open the doors in an attempt to cool down our tin can. Sometimes we would have to do a water service on the ground before take-off if the departure was delayed. I've had ice cubes on my neck just to cool myself down at times and given out cold cloths to passengers who looked like they were going to faint. In Jamaica we tended to joke that even their rainy days were sunny. They were home to the sun showers. Rain at destinations that didn't provide bridges or covered stairs caused an extra inconvenience, but most passengers didn't mind getting wet, especially if they were just starting their vacation.

Strong winds resulting in turbulence, especially persistently bumpy flights, were my nemesis. There were varying levels of turbulence, including light, moderate, and severe. During light turbulence flight attendants were still able to carry out their services, albeit a little choppy. Unless of course that flight attendant was me and I was still fairly new to flying, then you'd find me in the lavatory while my service trolley could be anywhere. I had a colleague who I used to fly with quite often who ended up nicknaming me Barfy. "Hey Barfy, you're looking a little green," she'd sometimes comment from across the aisle. I could handle light turbulence if it was short-lived; however, the never-ending rocking motion was what would do me in.

Moderate turbulence was more intense. Drinks got spilled, people bumped into things, and the seatbelt sign therefore got turned on. During this time, I would be strapped in my jump seat (with an airsickness bag in hand just in case). These were the times when many passengers would feel the need to now use the lavatories or grab something from the overhead bins or even toss their baby up and down in the air. Some would press the call light in hopes we'd risk our safety to grab them a drink, naive to the fact that we were buckled in as well so that we wouldn't get injured and be able to save their butts if an emergency were to occur.

In severe turbulence, the plane got tossed around as well as everything in it. These were the times people could get seriously hurt if not buckled in. I'd known a few flight attendants to get injured during this type of turbulence if there wasn't enough warning before it hit. Luckily, I'd never had to experience any severe turbulence without already being buckled in, and even then, it was short-lived. When I saw a colleague come to work wearing a wrist support and inquired as to what happened, she told me she had just returned from disability because her wrist broke during a sudden moment of in-flight turbulence. The flight attendants were in the middle of their services during a turnaround from the Caribbean when the seat-belt sign was turned on. As per standard, they stopped their services and proceeded to store their trolleys away, but unfortunately, they hit an air pocket before all of them could secure everything, including themselves. As the plane dropped a few feet, my friend hit the ceiling and ended up landing on top of her trolley and breaking her wrist. Turbulence could normally be predicted and avoided; however, clear air turbulence could hit out of nowhere, and suddenly there could be an explosive jolt in the plane and everything and everyone was being tossed around. I'd witnessed passengers cry, pray, vomit, and scream during severe turbulence, but luckily, in my experience, the worst of it was typically short-lived and even the panicked passengers would be able to relax once again. There wasn't much I could do except give them a look of reassurance from where I was seated. Unlike with moderate turbulence, no one dared attempt to stand during these times. When flight attendants said to keep seat-belts fastened at all times while seated, it was for good reason.

I would suggest making it a habit to always keep seat belts on when seated on an aircraft because you just never knew when sudden turbulence would occur. I'd never actually seen a passenger get injured because they ignored the seat-belt sign, but this was probably because we flight attendants would be yelling at them to immediately sit back down again and buckle up. Those who still refused to listen or pretended they couldn't hear us would sometimes get pointed out to everyone over the P.A. system. One of the more bolder flight attendants would usually say something like, "Ladies and gentlemen, this is a reminder to please stay seated with your seat belts fastened. This means you, too, passenger with the blue hoodie standing in the aisle. Thank you." At which point all the passengers would turn to see who this person was, and he or she would scooch back into their seat all embarrassed. Other times, passengers would dash to the lavatory before we had a chance to stop them or would flat out not care because they deemed it an "emergency," and all I could do was hope no one got hurt. Fortunately for those people, besides minor bumps, no one was ever injured that I knew of. Staying buckled was something I always did when travelling as a passenger, except I tended to forget that I was strapped in, so when I tried to get up, I'd be forced back down into my seat. If you knew that you got motion sickness on a plane, try sitting as close to the front as possible, since the back of the aircraft was always bumpier, and make sure you have at least one airsickness bag with you.

Even though incidents related to animals or insects were infrequent compared to storms and turbulence, they are still worth mentioning, as they did happen, nonetheless. I was surprised to know that bird strikes were common, as I only witnessed it once in all my years of flying. On one flight, my jump seat was directly next to the last door of the plane, and on take-off there was a bang and then I immediately saw feathers when I looked out the window. It reminded me of when my daughter came home upset one day because she had accidentally hit a bunny while driving, and when she looked in her rear-view mirror, all she saw was flying fluff.

When travelling to certain destinations we had to spray pesticides through the cabin before arrival to prevent the spread of insects and the diseases they could carry. (This disinfection was usually carried out prior to passenger boarding.) Despite this procedure, a stow away cockroach still managed to make an appearance on board. Luckily, another flight attendant was able to deal with this because my cup method may not have been effective. Even though I was not a fan of bugs, I still didn't like to kill them, so whenever I found one at home, I would place a plastic cup over it so my husband could deal with it once home. If I found one on the wall, I'd slide a piece of paper between the bug and the cup, and if I was feeling brave enough, I'd release it outside. Usually the cup got thrown outside along with the bug, but I always made sure to replace the cup and keep it handy on my window ledge.

The critical phases of a flight were during take-off and landing, so it was during these times that the flight attendant had to be extra vigilant and alert. They should be thinking of what to do in case of an emergency and possibly scoping out passengers who could be useful as ABPs.* During these critical times, the pilots couldn't be distracted from their flying duties and so the cockpit was sterile.* Everyone was focused on remaining safe. The different incidents that I'd dealt with on the job, such as mechanical issues, human error, natural disasters, and mother nature, were unfortunately still bound to happen no matter how well prepared everyone might be, but hopefully it was not something we couldn't go home and laugh about later.

*ABP (able-bodied passenger): This refers to someone who is able to assist in case of an emergency, preferably a flight crew member travelling as a passenger or else a fire fighter, a police officer, or military personnel. If none of these are available, then this passenger could be someone who at least looks strong and capable and is preferably cute.

*grounded: Not as in someone who is being punished and cannot leave home or someone who is emotionally and mentally stable, but rather this is when a plane (or even a flight crew member) is forced to remain on the ground and is not allowed to fly.

*holding pattern: This refers to the circling type maneuver an aircraft flies in when having to delay a landing above an airport.

*logbook: This is a record of all the maintenance work required and completed on an aircraft.

*sterile: Not as in someone who cannot produce children or something that is super clean and bacteria-free, but rather this is the condition in which a cockpit must be in during the critical phases of a flight, free of any non-essential activities or distractions.

Chapter Fourteen

The Advice

The job that I once thought would be a fun, temporary gig turned into a twenty-four-year career. I enjoyed being a flight attendant and living the sky life despite the demands of the job. I was grateful for all the knowledge and experience I'd gained working as a flight crew member, not to mention all the cool sights, foods, people, and stories I could talk or reminisce about. Over the course of my flying career, I was able to share advice and mantras related to the aviation world. The following was exactly that but with an Italian spin. Italians used proverbs as part of their communication, particularly in giving advice. Since I was raised in an Italian household, my way of thinking always reverted to those ingrained sayings. Some made sense, and I would later find myself using them on my own children, but others were simply weird. Even some Italian children's songs and nursery rhymes were quite bizarre. For the sake of this chapter, I attempted to unravel the cluster foxtrot of both wise and odd proverbs to pass on some sensible and sound advice in relation to flying.

The gift of a serving trolley as a child unknowingly ignited the spark in my becoming a flight attendant. After graduating university with no clear direction in a career choice, my path inevitably led me back to a serving trolley—an adult-sized one in the skies this time. It was a choice I would never regret. Lesson learned—do what makes you happy, and time will fly (literally if you become a flight attendant). Before I knew it, I was a lifer.

Much had changed in the physical appearance and requirements of flight attendants over the years, but they still managed to exude independence, confidence, and empathy with the help of that trusty smile. It also probably helped that they could tap into their "animal" personalities at a moment's notice to assist on the job. Because becoming a flight attendant was incredibly competitive, you should not expect to get hired on the first try, but, as my mother would say, *"chi la dura la vince."* Whoever persevered would win. In other words, if an airline passed on you, try again, even with a different airline, as long as you were not deluding yourself into thinking you met the height requirements when you were actually only 4'11" or believing they should still hire you even if you showed up in jeans and a t-shirt or even thought they would ignore your criminal record. If you tried again a second time and still did not get hired, *"non c'è due senza tre."* All good things came in threes. So, try again. When arriving for your interview, do as you should with all job interviews, stand tall and walk confidently, but most importantly, smile. Use your logic and common sense to answer their questions, but remember, *"in bocca chiusa non entra mosca."* Be careful of what you said. You shouldn't say anything that could be deemed as offensive or insensitive. There would be plenty of time for galley talk once you were hired.

I described the job of a flight attendant being like a new medical drug: life-altering but with numerous side effects, including physical pain, odours, flatulence, and sleep deprivation, to name a few. In short, flight attendants were underappreciated superheroes. Superheroes who could speak another language. If you didn't already speak a second language, now might be the time to learn. If applying in Canada, make sure you brushed up on your French. Being bilingual was a requirement with most Canadian airlines; although some might give you a grace period to learn it while on probation before testing you. It was time to go back to the days of *comment t'appelle tu* from core French class.

From all my years of flying, I'd put together a list of packing essentials when on the job. Besides the mandatory items required, such as an apron, gloves, and a safety vest, I would add a small sewing kit (you'd be surprised how many wardrobe malfunctions we had on board), a spare pair of nylons (unless you preferred to wear socks), spare pens, a hot water bottle (if on a red-eye), a reusable water bottle, medication, your emergency bag (if on a turn), toiletries (specifically deodorant, a toothbrush, and toothpaste), and food, lots of food. At the end of the day, what worked for one might not work for another, but it was always helpful to be prepared.

Flight attendants had to learn and master the art of balancing life at home with life in the skies. There were the natural stages in life, which, in my case, were dependent on whether I was single, married, or had younger or older children, and then there were the three typical work stages of a flight attendant. I revealed my own challenges and how I juggled them while in the skies, such as my pregnancies, my son's disease, and a forgetful husband. Lists were *my* saving grace. So my advice here was get your shit together and organize your own chaos if you wanted to succeed in both your home and sky life.

With being a flight attendant came annual training and exams. The scenarios and drills that I used as examples were what flight attendants had to do to demonstrate their skills and abilities to continue in their job. This included the use of the aircraft simulator, emergency equipment, and any other item or factor that could be associated with flying, including First Aid and CPR training. My advice, always volunteer to go second this way you could see what went right or wrong but then not have to sit and stress longer waiting for your turn. *"In bocca al lupo!"* In the mouth of the wolf. In other words, good luck!

There were different types of communication pertaining to aviation, including the flight attendant "sign language," the phonetic alphabet, acronyms, and abbreviations. This special lingo helped to facilitate services and communication as well as provided flight attendants with inflight entertainment. Being Italian helped me excel in the hand-gesturing department. Effective communication among flight attendants only worked if it was with those who were as experienced as you and therefore at the same level of aviation lingo. Not everyone would know why you were milking a cow in the middle of the aisle.

A flight attendant's commute was about the journey to work, which, for me, was dependent on the evolution of my appearance as a flight attendant. The challenges of being a flight attendant sometimes began even before boarding the plane, from the parking lot, to security, to the sometimes-long walks to the gate. My advice here would be to buy yourself a small car and always make sure you give yourself enough time to buy a coffee. Oh, and for the ladies, it helped to wear wire-free bras (unless you liked attention).

I shared my knowledge of the cabin on typical commercial planes, including how to find your seat, where the most comfortable area of a plane was according to your needs, and the all-important topic of how to use the lavatories, and I shared the different flight options available for both flight attendants and passengers. What I hoped that you learned here was if you wanted to be comfortable, have lots of personal space and privacy, and have a clean, luxurious lavatory on a plane, you shouldn't expect to find that flying economy on a commercial airline. And for all future flight attendants, *never* turn down a chance to work a ferry flight—you could thank me later.

A flight attendant's responsibilities were not limited to the ins and outs of a plane's interior or the ideal flight to take. The passengers—or the "specials"—were a big part of managing a life in the skies. They were the expecteds, unexpecteds, and the wannabes. When you finally earned your wings and joined the flight crew but then realized that the crazies *did*, in fact, exist in the skies and were not some imaginary group that flight attendants fabricated to be dramatic, you should keep this in mind: *"can che abbaia non morde."* A dog that barked didn't bite. Those same people who were yelling and threatening and making a huge fuss, usually over nothing of significance, were the least likely to take any action. Unless they'd been drinking, in which case, you should get backup because the intoxicated were unpredictable. You'd eventually learn which crazies you should listen to and try to assist and which you should ignore. Despite the drawbacks, such as the long hours, jet lag, stress, and having to smile even when being asked the most ridiculous questions, at the end of the flight, your job was done. You could step off that plane and go enjoy your sangria in Barcelona. You earned it.

Often, we saw passengers crying on the plane. They might have had a fear of flying, been missing someone, been travelling due to a loss, just watched a sad movie, or just been in pain from the air pressure or bad food. This was the time to be sympathetic. Even if you thought you were not doing anything, sometimes just being there to pass the tissue was usually enough. As Maya Angelou once said, "Try to be a rainbow in someone's cloud." I could have used a rainbow when I nearly died from wasabi overload.

Over the years I learned what proved to be most useful as carry-on items. What I would pack when working versus what I would pack when flying as a passenger were two different things. The following were some items you might want to pack as a passenger: a sweater, a travel pillow, headphones (preferably noise cancelling), flat shoes, a hot water bottle (if on a red-eye), a reusable water bottle, decongestant and acetaminophen, snacks, a large Ziploc (so you could store your trash and neatly hand it to the flight attendant at the end of the flight), a pen, and a book. If you also experienced motion sickness, you might want to bring along motion sickness pills, a change of clothes, antiseptic wipes, mints, a toothbrush, toothpaste, and a disposable plastic bag. As a tip, the airsickness bags on the plane were great for not only vomit but also for ice (in case of injury or to store medication), for garbage collection, and for carrying small items when you forgot a bag. My advice on proper packing might save you a little bit of embarrassment if you became one of the unexpected. It's not mandatory, but I think if more passengers flew prepared, it would definitely help make a flight attendant's job easier.

The customs hall was an inevitable part of flying internationally. Since going through customs was a process that even flight attendants had to endure, I offered insights and made suggestions to make it a little more tolerable, touching also upon the baggage claims area, the secondary hall, US pre-clear customs, and Nexus. Next time you had to go through customs, remember that *"le bugie hanno le gambe corte."* Lies had short legs. In other words, lying wouldn't get you far. This proverb was always a little odd to me because many Italians I knew did have short legs. I often wondered if that meant Italians lied a lot?

Just as flight attendants had to endure the customs process, so, too, did they have to learn how to deal with the many peeves of the job, including the ill-mannered passengers; unruly children; thoughtless parents; grievances over seats, baggage, and seat belts; and other smaller annoyances. Remember those galley tyrants I mentioned? They had to have listened to my mother's advice when she would say, *"chi fa da sé, fa per tre."* If you wanted something done right, you better do it yourself. It was best to stay out of their way, and no one would get hurt. You could ask the tyrants if they needed assistance, but when they inevitably shot you down, back away. Just like when dealing with passengers or crew on the aircraft, don't sweat the small stuff. Save your energy for the important matters. Anything else, *"che sarà sarà."* Whatever would be, would be. At the end of the day, you could hopefully leave those peeves behind you . . . or at least until your next flight.

To keep from being bored and lighten the mood, especially on long flights that sometimes involved many peeves, flight attendants kept laughter and humour at the forefront through playing games, creating challenges, and playing pranks. They would sometimes display fun and goofy attitudes with one another in their attempt to make each other laugh, both on and off the plane. And when all else failed, there was always crew drama to shake things up. You would learn how to work among many different personalities. You might have colleagues who you absolutely clicked with and had an amazing time working with, making your on-duty time just seem to fly. Then there were others whose personalities didn't quite jive with yours, and you were left constantly looking at how much time was left in the flight. The good news was your flight crew was constantly changing, so you might not see the same people for years. If you wanted to work with someone specific, you could always try requesting the same flight or switching with someone. If working with someone senior, however, keep this in mind: *"il lupo perde il pelo ma non il vizio."* You couldn't teach an old dog new tricks. Let them do their thing and roll with it. It was not worth agonizing over. If my mother insisted on mailing cheques to pay her bills, then *c'est la vie*. (Your first lesson in French words.) If all else failed, you could call your union rep.

The chapter on my many embarrassments was my selfless gift to you, where I shared embarrassing moments in both my personal and professional life. Even though it was more fun to laugh at others' humiliation, karma had a way of deflecting it back. (For more embarrassing moments on me, just write to my family—I'm sure they'd be more than happy to share.)

But it was probably the layovers that you found most interesting to learn about, as it was definitely something that drove flight attendants to pursue a life in the skies and was perhaps the best perk of the job. These layovers allowed me to connect with food (and bring home my favourites), explore and get lost, recharge, and travel with family (mishaps and all).

Me with my mother and older brother on my very first flight.

Even though my family liked to tease me about my extensive research and planning before going on vacation and my list of things to see and do, it had proved itself worthy, time and time again. It never hurt to read up on places you were visiting, especially when it was somewhere completely different than what you might be used to. As a matter of fact, it might even save you from overspending or experiencing disappointments. In all the times I had been to Paris, I had still only ever seen the Eiffel Tower from the base because tickets were always sold out, and I couldn't book in advance with the unpredictability of my job.

A little parting advice when on a layover, be careful who you chose to hang with because rumours spread quickly with flight crew, and you might just end up being the next galley topic. As my mother would say, *"dimmi con chi vai, e ti dirò chi sei."* This literally meant, tell me who you go with and I'll tell you who you are. In addition to that was the proverb *"meglio soli che mal accompagnati."* It was better to be alone than in bad company. This was especially true during your probationary period when the company could easily terminate your employment. You were one of the lucky ones to get hired as a flight attendant, so why would you want to jeopardize this?

Throughout this book, I stressed the importance of sufficient rest and the reality of flight attendants and sleep deprivation, both on overnight and day flights. The fatigue factor with flying was real, and as a flight attendant, you needed to develop an arsenal of survival tactics to stay awake. Despite best efforts, sometimes the tiredness would account for a flight attendant's not-so-pristine appearance, clumsiness, and unwarranted giggles. My advice here, sleep when you could and drink coffee, lots and lots of coffee. Being well rested and caffeine ready would also prove useful when dealing with the many unforeseen incidents that happened on duty, including mechanical issues, human error, disasters, and mother nature herself. The delays and cancellations that might result could have both positive and negative effects, depending on your situation at the time. As they said, shit happened.

I've tried to pass on the more relevant proverbs that made sense relative to being a flight attendant, but there were many that left me shaking my head and wondering *why*, just like the following nursery rhyme from my mother's hometown of Brescia:

Piero, Piero l'è nàt a fa l'erba
èl sé mpignit le braghe dè merda
la so mama l'è nada a töl
la sé mpignida èl bigaröl

Peter, Peter went to cut the grass
he filled his pants with shit
his mom went to get him
she filled up her apron (with shit)

As a final piece of advice, you should just have fun, even if that meant photobombing passengers. If you weren't happy, fake it. Put on that flight attendant smile and remember, *"dopo la pioggia, arriva il sole."* After the rain came sunshine, so things were bound to improve (except in Jamaica where there was always sun). And if you were the passenger, *"l'ospite è come il pesce, dopo tre giorni puzza."* A guest was like a fish, after three days it stank. In other words, when you arrived at your destination and you heard "thanks for flying with us," that meant "get out." You might have also heard the flight director on the P.A. say, "Whoever is last off will have to clean the plane." We weren't kidding. Don't lollygag, use the bathroom, take more pictures, and try to make small talk with the crew. Just get out. (This was like when I'd put on my pyjamas if I was home and I wanted my guests to leave but didn't want to straight out tell them.)

My life experiences, whether embarrassing or proud, joyful or sad, made me who I was—an introverted Canuck with kinetosis who was a nerdy wife, tough mudder, and judgy flight attendant. I'd made some poor choices in life—like crawling through mud under barbed wire, running up at least three ridiculously steep ski hills, plunging into freezing water, and getting electrocuted by live wires all while on heavy pain medication due to putting my back out just so I could get a headband—but becoming a flight attendant was not one of them. As much as I might have wanted to pop a slide and run off onto the tarmac at times, I was glad I chose to stick around instead. Now please remove your red warning tag, leave all your woes and troubles behind, return to your economy seat, leave me the foxtrot alone, and have a nice day (all said with a smile, of course).

The End

Acknowledgements

First and foremost, I'd like to thank my husband, Joe, for keeping me true to my word on someday writing a book. Without his repetitive and annoying questioning—"so how's that book coming along?"—this book would not exist. Once the book was finished, though, he told me he'd prefer to wait for the audio version rather than read it himself.

Thank you to my three children, Shannon, Sarah, and Adam, for being old enough to fend for themselves and know when to steer clear of me.

Thanks to my dog, Bello, for always being by my side and keeping me company—except if he was being offered food, or a squeaky toy to play with, or to go for a walk.

A huge thanks to my editor, Melissa McCoubrey, who magically transformed my jumbled mess into something that made sense. Your patience and input were invaluable.

To my family and friends, thanks for encouraging and believing in me even when I wanted to throw in the towel.

And, finally, thank you to my readers, who know how to make excellent choices in reading material.

About the Author

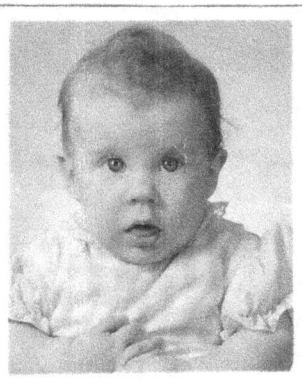

Barbara's first passport picture

Barbara Borzi is a Canuck introvert who is afraid of heights and suffers from motion sickness so, naturally, she decided to become a flight attendant. She managed to turn what was supposed to be a fun, temporary job into an unforgettable lifetime career full of stories, adventures, and the occasional tears and vomit. Barbara and her husband currently share their home in Brampton, Ontario with their three children, and spoiled dog.

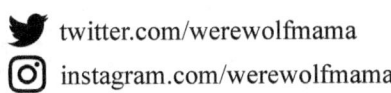

twitter.com/werewolfmama
instagram.com/werewolfmama

www.ingramcontent.com/pod-product-compliance
Lightning Source LLC
Chambersburg PA
CBHW071840080526
44589CB00012B/1062